THE
ART OF
WISDOM

BALTASAR GRACIÁN

Camelot
EDITORA

GET TO KNOW OUR
BOOKS BY ACCESSING HERE!

4th Printing 2023

President: Paulo Roberto Houch
MTB 0083982/SP

Editorial Coordination: Paola Houch and Priscilla Sipans
Translation: Francine Cervato
English text review: Daniel Rabbers
Art Coordination: Rubens Martim (cover)
Text Preparation: Fabio Kataoka
Review: Aline Ribeiro
Layout: Rogério Pires

Sales: Phone: +55 (11) 3393-7727

(comercial2@editoraonline.com.br) The legal deposit was made.

International Cataloging in Publication (CIP) data according to ISBD	
C181a	**Camelot Editora**
	Art Of Wisdom / Camelot Editora. – Barueri : On Line Editora, 2024. 128 p. ; 15,1cm x 23cm.
	ISBN: 978-65-6095-162-4
	1. Art. I. Title.
2024-4117	CDD 700 CDU 7

Elaborated by Vagner Rodolfo da Silva - CRB-8/9410

IBC — Instituto Brasileiro de Cultura LTDA
CNPJ 04.207.648/0001-94
Avenida Juruá, 762 – Alphaville Industrial ZIP
CODE: 06455-010 – Barueri/SP
www.editoraonline.com.br

PREFACE

The art of wisdom.

That is an intriguing title, don't you think?

In case you have not found any reason for strangeness in this so-called "Art of Wisdom", I feel compelled to justify mine.

Both the word art and the word wisdom can house more than one meaning. These are concepts that deserve, each one, a lot of ink. And not a few treaties.

In this way, for the one who takes on the responsibility of writing the preface to this work, this title alone is already "enough". The temptation is great to evacuate the problem in the simplest way. Some paragraphs about art, others about wisdom and... voilà, mission accomplished..

But these two letters "of", which are uniting "art" and "wisdom", these, indeed, suggest greater difficulty. After all, the author did not write two texts, one about art and the other about wisdom. He also did not bring them together with a simple "and". He made a point of this "of". Without examining its meaning, we cannot know what the book is about. Simple as that.

We are left, then, to face the following question: when we state that one thing belongs to another, as in the case of the art of wisdom, what exactly do we mean?

The reading of this preface will be lighter if we investigate this meaning in other, less abstract expressions, and with the same structure: that is, that also use the preposition of, whether or not merged with the article the, but between nouns, let's say, more palpable.

Let's start, then, at random, with "the house of Joan". As we know, she gave birth to twins and – embracing popular expressions here once and for all – she was immortalized as a mother, in addition to being the owner of her house.

Now, "the house of mother Joan" indicates that the house belongs to her. We are talking about possession or property.

The initiative was sympathetic, but I suppose that is not what Baltasar thought when defining the title of his book. Wisdom as the owner of art. It gets weird. It does not seem to be the case.

A little different is the meaning of "the sleeve of the jacket". What is intended to be indicated in this second expression is the part (sleeve) in the face of the whole (jacket).

The art of wisdom, in this case, would indicate the specific piece of wisdom, namely art. In this sense, the work would be an essay about art. As much as a text with the title "the sleeve of the jacket" would have as its object the sleeve.

Now, reading the first few pages is enough to disprove the hypothesis. That is not what this is about.

We find the same construction mediated by the preposition of in "pie made of pumpkin". In this case, the pumpkin does not own the pie. Nor a part of it. But this one is made from it, having it as the master ingredient.

There are two neighboring meanings here: of constitution and of origin. The pie is made of pumpkin, in the sense of what constitutes it, or, the same pie made from pumpkin, which is not exactly the same thing.

In both cases, we do not gain clarity to explain what our author meant. Between art and wisdom, one is not made of the other. Following this semantic path, art would be made of wisdom or from it.

One could always force the hand here and there. But, even if we managed to find links with some elegance, there would be no gain, beyond the most obvious. Of what we have known forever.

What art has to do with wisdom. Both can appear together in some sentence. After all, wisdom is thinking about life, when that life is human. And art can also have this same life as inspiration. But then one being made of the other is another thing. And writing an entire book based on this hypothesis suggests raising the bet, without fear.

What is certain is that we are still far from what was going on in the author's mind to have chosen this title. But we will not give up so easily.

Let us find other possible meanings in the use of that structure. For example, in "a book of geography". In this case, the preposition of indicates purpose. A book to teach geography. An instrument used for this.

This meaning, applied to art and wisdom, requires adaptation. The conversion of the second term into a verb. Knowing instead of wisdom. And we would have the art of knowing, therefore..

In the case of a purpose, the author's art would be for knowledge. Used for knowledge. Intended to knowledge. Aimed at the practice of knowledge. An instrument of knowledge.

Of everything that was said so far, this seems to be, at first glance, the most plausible meaning.

But the reader will have noticed the initial pirouette. Exchanging wisdom for knowledge — as if there were no semantic aggression in this exchange — was what allowed us this breath of apparent relevance.

Certainly, art can be an instrument of learning and knowledge. Aristotle saw the imitation of fragments of the world implemented by painting and sculpture, for example, as a magnificent pedagogical resource. But Baltasar's book is not about that. At all.

When you think about art, maybe the so-called fine arts come to mind. Painting, sculpture, music, poetry, architecture, dance. And there will be those who go further, including theater, romance, cinema and others.

There is in all art the gestation of something beyond artistic activity. As in the Greek concept of poiesis. An action that causes something to emerge outside of it. Beyond it.

Thus, the canvas goes beyond the handling of the brush, the sculpture that is different in relation to the sculpted matter, the song that surpasses the composer's work, the building that is more than its project, and so on. It is a work. A work of art. From a piece of matter transformed by man through a set of interventions with certain specific characteristics.

This activity is strictly human. In artistic production there is an awareness of its process supposedly absent among non- human living beings.

The bird called Rufous hornero makes its home. Bees and ants also build their shelters. But architecture, as art, cannot be confused with these strictly instinctive movements of non- human animality.

Nature, in fact, is not an artist. Even though it is beautiful. Incomparable. Unsurpassed in beauty. Like the sunset, which was not made by man.

But art was not always just a fine art. The word comes from Latin, which in Greek was called tekhné, a set of instruments and knowledge suitable for achieving a certain previously established result.

The meaning of these terms, art and technique, evolved in parallel and in progressive distancing. Technique started distinguishing itself more and more from art due to its impersonality.

A technical instrument can be manufactured by anyone, following a protocol using appropriate resources. The same does not happen with a work of art. Maybe this is why the artist's work is evaluated by the ruler of sensitivity, while the technician's work is evaluated by the efficiency of what he or she produced.

What is certain is that all art can make us think about innovation, about transgression, about the avant-garde. And, in this case, we would be much closer to what our author's work intends. A reflection about life, in its multiple situations and scenarios, which aims to break with a certain common sense of the time. This interpretation does not clash with what is presented and discussed in the work and seems, finally, to shed some light on the spirit of its author.

Art can also make us think about beauty. In everything that is beautiful. And, in this case, Baltasar would be denouncing the beauty of life when governed by intelligence, conditioned by the use of a certain reason, that is, in the light of a certain wisdom. The semantic bet is not absurd, although much of what the book suggests has more to do with "not getting too bad" than with living life beautifully.

Well, editorial limits require me to say goodbye. No proofs of theorems or conclusions to write down in a notebook.

As if this lack of certainty was not enough, nothing was said here about Baltasar. His life, his work, his ideas. The numbers of strokes, words and pages require short covering choices. And prefaces do not have clear recipes. I therefore chose to problematize the title of the work.

The author's biographical information, always extremely important for a good understanding of what he wrote, can be easily found with a couple of clicks.

Our Baltasar Gracián was a Jesuit and lived in the first half of the 16th century. And this is very relevant. The rest is up to you. Good research and good reading of this fascinating book.

Clóvis de Barros Filho
Speaker, writer and presenter

INTRODUCTION

The three hundred maxims or aphorisms, by Baltasar Gracián, became known in English as *The Art of Wisdom – Pocket Oracle and Art of Prudence* or *The Art of Prudence*. The original title of the work, in Spanish, is *Oráculo Manual y Arte de Prudencia*.

The book was published in 1647 and remains current and inspiring until nowadays, after more than 370 years. These are guidelines for evolving as a human being and living fully. The teachings do not have a religious or spiritual nature. They bring simple and short philosophical considerations that can be read in sequence or randomly.

There are few documents about the life of Baltasar Gracián. Some researchers concluded that he was the son of a large family without many resources, despite his father being a doctor. Many of his brothers died as children.

Baltasar continued his studies with the guidance of an uncle, who was a chaplain in the city of Toledo. Thus, at the age of eighteen, he entered the Society of Jesus very prepared, where he was a brilliant student and became rector of the Jesuit college located in Tarragona.

Baltasar Gracián was a great observer of human nature and the tricks of power, which he exposed with great conciseness and lucidity in his works. A philosopher and a literate man, he was a grammar teacher and wrote seven books, some on the style and art of writing and others criticizing society at the time, which were initially published under pseudonyms.

1

EVERYTHING CAN COME TO PERFECTION, AND BECOMING A TRUE PERSON IS THE GREATEST PERFECTION OF ALL

Nowadays, more is required of a single wise man than in the past of seven. It now takes more resources to deal with a single man than with an entire people in the past.

2

CHARACTER AND INTELLIGENCE

It is the characteristics that make the qualities shine - one without the other brings only partial happiness. It is not enough to be intelligent, it is also necessary to have character. The fool fails because they disregard their condition, position, origin and friendships.

3

KEEP THE SUSPENSE

The surprise of success leads to admiration. Revealing the entire strategy is neither useful nor enjoyable. When you avoid attracting immediate attention, you arouse curiosity, especially in relation to important subjects that generate expectations. Mystery causes reverence. Even when revealing yourself, it is best to avoid total frankness and not allow everyone to know your inner self. It is in cautious silence that prudence takes refuge. Decisions, once declared, are not valued as they should and cause criticism. In case of failure, the result is twice as bad. To keep people's attention and interest, keep the mystery, following the example of divine wisdom.

4

KNOWLEDGE AND COURAGE COME TOGETHER FOR GREATNESS

Being immortal qualities, they can immortalize man. We are what we know, therefore the wise ones are capable of anything. A man without knowledge is a world in the dark. Discernment and strength are like eyes and hands: without them, wisdom is sterile.

5

CREATE DEPENDENCE

What makes an image sacred is not the art of those who create it, but the faith of those who worship it. The intelligent ones prefer the needy to the grateful. Vulgar gratitude is worth less than polite hope, because hope has a good memory, and gratitude does not. There is more to be gained from lack than from courtesy. The one who has already quenched their thirst, turns their back to the well, and the squeezed orange turns from gold to mud. Once the need is satisfied, good manners and appreciation disappear. The most important lesson that experience teaches is to inspire confidence & safety and nurture them, always nourishing them, without ever satisfying them, preserving the need for self in others. However, one should never go to the extreme of remaining silent to mislead others, nor make the damage of others irreparable for one's own benefit.

6

REACH PERFECTION

No one is born perfect: it is necessary to improve yourself daily, both in your personal and professional life, until you become complete, full of gifts and qualities. People must be recognized for their refined taste, their acute intelligence, their purity of intention, their capacity for discernment. Some are never complete, they are always missing something, while others take a long time to do so. The perfect man, wise in expression and prudent in actions is accepted, and even desired, in the select group of prudent ones.

7

DO NOT SHINE MORE THAN YOUR BOSS

Every defeat causes hatred, and surpassing your boss is as foolish as it is fatal. Supremacy is always hated, especially by hierarchical superiors. It is possible to hide talent and ability in the same way that beauty is disguised with a skilled touch of carelessness. There are many that do not mind being surpassed in wealth, character or temper, but no one, especially those in a leadership position, likes to be surpassed in talent. It is, after all, the king of attributes, and any crime against it constitutes lese majesty. Sovereigns want to be bigger in what matters most. Princes like to be helped, but not overcome. When you give someone advice, do it as if you are reminding them of something they forgot, not as if you are explaining something they are unable to understand. Stars teach us such subtlety: although bright, they never dare to surpass the brightness of the sun.

8

DO NOT GIVE IN TO PASSIONS

One of the highest spiritual qualities is not giving in to fleeting passions. Passion may even affect you, but do not allow it to affect your position, much less if it is important. It is a sensible way to avoid problems and a shorter way to gain the esteem of others.

9

SOFTEN THE TYPICAL DEFECTS OF YOUR COUNTRY

Water shares the good and bad qualities of the beds it runs through; men share them from the region in which they were born. Some owe more than others to their country or hometown, as they were born in a favorable land. No country, not even the most cultured, is without a typical defect, and such weaknesses serve as consolation or defense to neighboring nations. Correcting, or at least disguising, such flaws is already a triumph. By doing this, you will be recognized as special among your people, as the unexpected is always more valued. Certain defects are caused by lineage, condition, occupation and age. When the same person brings together all these defects and does not want to take the trouble to correct them, it ends up becoming an unbearable monster.

10

FORTUNE AND FAME

What one has as fickle, the other has as firm. The first helps us to live, the second helps us later. Fortune against envy; fame against oblivion. We can desire fortune and even build it with our efforts, but fame requires constant work. The desire for reputation comes from virtue: fame was and is the sister of giants. Always walk between extremes: monsters or prodigies, boos or applause.

11

ALLY YOURSELF WITH PEOPLE WHO CAN TEACH

Make friendly convivial a school of erudition, and conversation a means of learning. Make friends with your teachers and combine the useful (learning) with the pleasant (the exchange of ideas). Intersperse teaching with instruction: what you say will be rewarded with applause; what you hear, with learning. What leads us towards others, in general, is our own convenience; which must be ennobled. The cautious ones frequent the houses of renowned men, which are theaters of greatness, not palaces of futility. Some are famous for their knowledge, common sense, example and way of acting and are oracles of wisdom. Those who accompany them form a refined academy of discretion and common sense.

12

NATURE AND ART, MATTER AND WORK

Every beauty needs help. If it is not ennobled by art, perfection becomes atrocity. Art recovers what is bad and perfects what is good. Nature often fails us when we need it most, so let us turn to art. Without it, even the greatest talent is crude. Without culture, even perfection turns into mediocrity. Without art, man appears brutish and rude: perfection can only be achieved through polishing.

13

REALIZE SECOND INTENTIONS

Men's lives consist of a struggle against the malice of others. Cunning arms itself with stratagems of ill intention: it never does what it says, misleads and then attacks suddenly, always attentive and ready to confuse. In order to gain attention and trust, it insinuates an intention to then change position and win by surprise. Perceptive intelligence avoids cunning by observing it closely, spying on it cautiously, understanding the opposite of what cunning implies and immediately identifying false intentions. Intelligence ignores the first intention, awaiting the second and even the third. The simulation grows even more when it sees its trick discovered and tries to deceive by telling the truth. It changes the game, deceives with its apparent lack of malice. Its cunning is based on the greatest sincerity. However, observation moves forward, sees through it all and discovers the shadows wrapped in light. It deciphers the intention, which, the simpler it is, the more cunning it is. This is how the cunning of Python fights against the clarity of Apollo's rays.

14

REALITY AND MANNER

The content is not enough, the format is also necessary. Lack of education can even make you lose your mind. Good manners fix everything: they soften a no, sweeten the truth and make even old age to seem beautiful. The way of doing things is very important, courtesy wins everyone's affection. Education is very precious. Speak and behave well and you will be capable of overcoming any difficult situation.

15

HAVE COMPETENT ALLIES

The powerful ones are victorious because they have intelligent people close to them, with remarkable understanding, capable of freeing them from troubles in which they are placed by their own ignorance and of taking their place in the fight against difficulties. Knowing how to take advantage of wise allies is a unique quality: better than enslaving kings. It is a much better way to dominate others: skillfully turn into allies those that nature endowed with superior intelligence. We have a short time to live and a lot to learn, and we cannot live without knowing. It takes remarkable skill to learn effortlessly: have the advice of wise men at your disposal and make their speech your own. If you act like this, you will speak for many, in any meeting, as your words will be those of the wise men who advised you and you will gain fame thanks to the sweat of others. Choose a topic and allow those around you to provide you with concentrated knowledge. If you cannot make knowledge your servant, make it your ally.

16

KNOWLEDGE AND GOOD INTENTIONS

They guarantee the fruits of your success. When intelligence joins with evil intentions, there is not an alliance, but a monstrous violation that poisons the best qualities. Aided by knowledge, it corrupts with more subtlety. Unhappy is the man endowed with intelligence and courage who gives himself over to evil! Science without good judgment is even worse.

17

ACT IN A VARIED WAY

This confuses others, especially rivals. If you always act the same way, your intentions will be anticipated and frustrated. It is easy to shoot the bird that flies straight, but not the one that changes its flight path. Do not always act according to your goals, or follow the same strategy twice, and others will not realize the trick. Malice lies in wait - it takes great cunning to deceive it. The perfect player never moves the piece that is expected, much less the one its opponent wants.

18

EFFORT AND TALENT

There is no perfection without these two qualities. Having both, it is possible to overcome yourself. A mediocre diligent person is better than a negligent gifted person. Work dignifies. With it, you acquire reputation. Some are unable to apply themselves even to the simplest tasks, as the effort almost always depends on personality. It is acceptable to be mediocre in an unimportant job: we can excuse ourselves by saying that we were cut out for nobler things. However, there is no excuse for being content with being mediocre in a superior task, even though you can be excellent in the simplest. Both art and nature are necessary, and effort completes them.

19

DO NOT CREATE VERY HIGH EXPECTATIONS

Anything that is highly idealized rarely lives up to expectations. Reality does not compare to imagination, because imagining perfection is easy, achieving it is hard. The union of imagination and desire always creates things much better than they actually are. No matter how great the qualities are, they will never be enough to satisfy expectations, and those who feed them too much are more likely to be disappointed than to make their dreams come true. Hope can be treacherous; common sense must balance it, trying to make the gratification for the result greater than the desire. A good reputation initially serves to arouse curiosity, not to sell the idea. It is much better when reality exceeds expectations, and something turns out to be better than we imagined. This rule does not apply to evil. When one exaggerates expectations of misfortune, one celebrates when reality arrives, and what was feared as disastrous comes to seem tolerable.

20

LIVE IN THE RIGHT TIME

People of imminent merit depend on the time in which they live to make use of them. Not everyone lived at the right time, and many of those who did were unable to take advantage of their time. Some deserved better times, but not everything that is good always triumphs. All things have their time, even qualities are subject to fashion. However, wisdom has an advantage: it is eternal. If this is not your century, many others will be.

21

THE ART OF BEING FORTUNATE

Fortune has its rules and, for the wise ones, not everything depends on chance: it counts on the help of effort. Some are content to rely on luck. Others are more sensible and act on their own, with a cautious audacity that, supported by courage and virtue, pursues luck with the purpose of obtaining the desired results. However, the true wise man has a single plan of action: virtue and prudence; because there is no such thing as luck or bad luck, but rather prudence or precipitation.

22

BE WELL-INFORMED

Wise ones arm themselves with enchanting, practical and current erudition, more informative than vulgar. They know how to use witty phrases and gallant attitudes at the appropriate time. Advice is better conveyed jokingly than instructed seriously. For some, knowledge gained through conversation is more important than all seven arts, regardless of how liberal they are.

23

DOMINATE THE DEFECTS

There are few people who do not have some defect, weakness or character flaw, which they give in to even when it would be easy to dominate them. The prudence of others is distressed when it sees a sublime, universal talent threatened by a small defect: a single cloud covers the sun. Flaws are stains on the face of reputation, and malevolence quickly notices them. It takes great skill to transform them into signs of beauty. In this way, Caesar, the Roman leader, knew how to cover his baldness with a laurel wreath.

24

CONTROL IMAGINATION

We must sometimes stimulate and sometimes restrain imagination. Happiness depends on imagination, which must be governed by common sense. Sometimes it behaves like a tyrant: it is not enough to speculate, it comes into action and dominates our lives, making it pleasant or unpleasant, leaving us unhappy or too satisfied with ourselves. For some, it causes disgust; to others, it promises happiness, adventure and joy. It can do all this, if it is not restrained by reason and prudence.

25

BE A GOOD UNDERSTANDER

Knowing how to argue was once the art of arts, but today it is not enough: we need to be fortune-tellers, especially on issues that can deceive us. To be understood, you have to be a good understander. There are people who guess feelings and see hidden intentions. The truths that interest us most are only half revealed; only those who are attentive understand them completely. In matters that seem favorable to you, do not be too credulous; in unfavorable ones, let go of the reins.

26

FIND THE WEAK POINT OF EACH ONE

The art of influencing the will of others is more a matter of skill than determination. It is necessary to understand the other's mind. Each person has their object of affection, which varies according to taste. Everyone idolizes something: love, money or, most of the time, pleasure. The trick is knowing how to identify the motivation of each individual. It is like holding the key to other people's desires. It is necessary to achieve basic motivation, which is not always something high and important.

It is almost always something insignificant, since there are more disordered people in the world than there are disciplined ones. First of all, evaluate the character and then touch on the weak point. Put it to the test by insisting on it and you will infallibly defeat it.

27

IT IS BETTER TO BE INTENSE THAN EXTENSIVE

Perfection is not in quantity, but in quality. Everything that is good is rare, and what is abundant is vulgar. Even among men, there are many small-minded giants. Some praise the books for their size, as if they were written to exercise the arms, not the intelligence. The volume by itself is nothing special, and it is a very common mistake to try to know everything, as you can end up without mastering any subject in depth. Depth leads to excellence and, in matters of great importance, to fame.

28

NEVER BE COMMON

Especially in taste. Wise is the one who does not accept what pleases the majority; the discreet are not satisfied with common applause. Some people are fools, chameleons of popularity who take more pleasure in the breath of the crowd than in the gentle breezes of Apollo. The wise man is also not vulgar in his discernment; he does not appreciate the miracles of the majority, which are nothing more than charlatanism. The crowd pays attention to foolishness and does not pay attention to good advice.

29

INTEGRITY AND FIRMNESS

Always be on the side of reason, with such firmness of purpose that neither common passion nor tyrannical violence will divert you from it. However, where to find this balance point? Few are dedicated to integrity: many praise it, but few practice it. Some follow it until the situation becomes difficult, when the fake ones deny it and the politicians just simulate it. The upright ones are not afraid to oppose friendship, power and their own convenience. The cunning ones make subtle excuses and speak of laudable motives or reasons of state, but the truly loyal man considers dissimulation a kind of betrayal; he prides himself more on being firm than shrewd, and is always on the side of truth. If he differs from others, it is not because of any whim of his own, but because others abandoned the truth.

30

DO NOT DEDICATE YOURSELF TO UNIMPORTANT THINGS

Much less to imaginary subjects, which cause more contempt than prestige. Whims lead in many directions, and it is necessary to escape from all of them. A sensible person must avoid fanaticism and eccentricities, as these, although they may lead to fame, more often provoke laughter than respect. Even when seeking wisdom, the cautious must avoid affectation and public attention, especially in matters where they may seem ridiculous.

31

SEEK THE FORTUNATE ONES AND AVOID THE UNFORTUNATE ONES

There is no feeling more contagious than unhappiness. Never open the door to the lesser of evils, as many others – greater – lie in wait outside. The secret to the game is knowing how to deal the cards: the worst card in the winning hand in front of you is more important than the best card in the losing hand you just bet on. When in doubt, approach the wise and the cautious ones. Sooner or later, luck will come to them.

32

BE KNOWN FOR PLEASING OTHERS

For rulers, it is useful to obtain good graces of everyone: the only advantage of a sovereign is to have more opportunities than others to do good. Those who are friends make friends. Others, on the contrary, decide not to please; not because it is laborious, but out of evil, opposed to divine goodness.

33

KNOW HOW TO DODGE

One of the most important skills in life is knowing how to say no, whether in business or in private life. There are certain non-essential activities that consume very precious time, and busying yourself with the trivial is worse than doing nothing. It is not enough not to meddle in other people's affairs: you must also prevent others from meddling in yours. Do not give yourself to others to the point of forgetting yourself. Do not abuse your friends or ask them for more than they give you of free initiative, as all exaggeration is negative, especially in relationships. With this moderation, you will remain in others' good graces and retain their respect. Therefore, maintain the freedom to choose what you prefer and never harm yourself.

34

CULTIVATE YOUR BEST GIFT

Value your best quality and improve the others. Everyone would be successful if they knew what they excelled at. Identify your strengths and dedicate yourself to improving them diligently. Some are especially insightful or brave. Others do violence to intelligence and therefore stand out in nothing. They let themselves be blinded and flattered by their own passions until, too late, time disproves them.

35

ANALYZE THE QUESTIONS CAREFULLY

Reflect mainly on the most relevant ones. Foolish ones make mistakes because they do not think: they do not really reflect on most things and, because they do not realize the advantages or disadvantages, they do not use their efforts well. Some think in reverse, paying a lot of attention to what matters little, and little attention to what matters most. Many people never lose their reason because they have no reason to lose. There are certain things that we must consider carefully and keep rooted in our minds. The wise ones pay attention to everything, but they only dig where there is gold. They make reflection go beyond perception.

36

EVALUATE LUCK

To be capable of acting and committing, it is more important to think than to moderate temper. The fool always asks for calm instead of prudence. Knowing how to manage luck is an art, whether waiting for it, as it sometimes takes a while to come, or taking advantage of it, when it is favorable, no matter how much you do not understand its mysteries. If luck has been on your side, proceed boldly, as it appreciates the bold ones. If, on the contrary, you find yourself in a streak of bad luck, wait. Withdraw to avoid double failure. If you controlled yourself, you took a big step forward.

37

DECIPHER AND
USE INSINUATION

It is the most delicate point in human relationships. It can be used to test common sense and discreetly probe the heart. There is the malicious, reckless insinuation, dyed with the claws of envy, stained with the poison of passion: an invisible lightning capable of taking away all grace and esteem from us. Many lost friendships due to a single offensive insinuation; even those who did not suffer the slightest shock when exposed to vulgar talk and individual malevolence. Other insinuations, because they are favorable, act on the contrary, sustaining and supporting our reputation. It is necessary to parry the darts as skillfully as the bad intention throws them: receive them with care, wait for them with caution. A good defense requires knowledge. A blow delivered against a forewarned target will always frustrate.

38

LEAVE THE GAME WHILE YOU
HAVE AN ADVANTAGE

A strategic withdrawal is as important as a brave offensive. Keep great achievements safe, as it is necessary to be suspicious when good luck lasts. It is safer when luck alternates with bad luck, which, above all, makes it possible to savor and value victories. When luck lasts too long, the greater the chances of losing everything. Sometimes, luck compensates us by exchanging the short duration for the intensity of the joy it gives us. It gets tired when it has to carry someone on its back for a long time.

39

TAKE ADVANTAGE OF THE MAXIMUM POINT

Works of nature have their peak or point of perfection. Until they reach that point, they are on the rise and then decline. Rare are the works of art that cannot be improved. Those who have good taste know how to enjoy everything to its maximum point. Not everyone can do it, and not everyone who can knows how to do it. Even the fruits of understanding reach the perfect point of ripeness. However, it is necessary to know how to recognize it, to be able to value and take advantage of it.

40

EARN THE ESTEEM OF EVERYONE

It is great to arouse admiration, but even better is to earn esteem. This depends, in part, on favorable circumstances; the rest is effort. Qualities and attributes are not enough, although, in general, it is easier to earn affection when you already have a good reputation. Benevolence depends on beneficence. Do all kinds of good: kind words and good deeds. Love, if you want to be loved. It is with courtesy that great men captivate others. First the acts and then the words. From sword to paper, for the sympathy of writers is eternal.

41

NEVER EXAGGERATE

Do not use superlatives. Generally, they do not correspond to the truth and cast doubt on your ability to discern. By exaggerating, we waste our praise and reveal a lack of knowledge and taste. Praise awakens curiosity, which generates desire, and, later, when it is discovered that something or someone was overestimated, as often happens, expectations are frustrated, the object of praise is devalued and the person who praised it loses its credibility. The cautious ones show restraint, preferring to sin by lack rather than by excess. True eminences are rare, so moderate your appreciation. Overvaluing something or someone is a form of lie that can ruin your reputation for good taste and, even worse, for wisdom.

42

NATURAL LEADERSHIP

It is a superior, secret force that originates from a natural gift and not from artificiality. Everyone succumbs to it without knowing why, recognizing the secret force and vigor of natural authority. Such individuals have a proud character: they are natural leaders. They earn the respect, hearts and even minds of other people. When blessed with other gifts, they become excellent political organizers, capable of accomplishing more with a simple insinuation than others can with a long-winded speech.

43

FEEL WISE AND TALK AS THE PEOPLE

Rowing against the current does not undo mistakes and is very dangerous. Only Socrates could afford to try. Disagreement is taken as an insult, as it condemns the opinion of others, and many take the pain of those they believe to be unfairly criticized or resent of those they believe to be unfairly praised. Truth belongs to few, and deception is as common as it is vulgar. Wise men are not known by what they say in public, because they do not talk with their own voice, but with the voice of general ignorance, although in their hearts they abhor it. The sensible man avoids both refuting and being refuted. His judgment may be one of censorship, but he will avoid publicizing it. Opinion is free and should not be violated. He withdraws into sacred silence and, if he makes comments, it is for the few and sensible ones.

44

BE SYMPATHETIC WITH GREAT MEN

Having the ability to coexist with heroes is commendable. This gift, called sympathy, is a wonder of nature, as it is as mysterious as it is beneficial. There is kinship of heart and temper, and the effects of sympathy resemble those which vulgar ignorance attributes to magic potions. Sympathy, in addition to helping us gain fame, makes others lean towards us, quickly earning their goodwill. It is capable of persuading without words, conquering without merit. There is active and passive sympathy, and both work wonders among those who have a prominent position. It is necessary to have the ability to know them, distinguish them and take advantage of them. There is not enough effort if there is not this privilege.

45

USE INDIRECT ROUTES WITHOUT ABUSE

And, above all, do not reveal them, as all art must be disguised so as not to arouse suspicion, especially hidden intentions, which are hateful. Deceit is common, so be careful. However, do not let others see your caution, so that they do not lose trust and feel insulted, which generates revenge, which awakens unimaginable evil. Acting thoughtfully gives us a great advantage; there is no greater food for discourse. The greatest perfection of an action depends on the perfection with which we execute it.

46

MODERATE YOUR ANTIPATHY

We often instinctively hate someone, even before we know their qualities, and it is common for this aversion to turn against eminent people.

May your wisdom control this feeling, as there is nothing worse than anger directed against those who are superior. Just as it is commendable to have sympathy for heroes, it is despicable to treat them with antipathy.

47

RUN AWAY FROM DIFFICULTIES

This is one of the main rules of wisdom. The path to achieve great things is long and prudent people remain in the middle, in balance and common sense. Only after much consideration do they reach a decision, as it is much better to be safe than sorry. Dangerous situations threaten common sense, and it is safer to avoid them. One danger usually leads to another greater one, and so on, until the edge of the precipice. Some people, by temper or training, are reckless and hasty and easily get involved in complicated or risky situations, but those who are guided by the light of reason evaluate the situation and conclude that it is more sensible to avoid danger than to overcome it. If you are faced with a reckless fool, try not to be another one.

48

HAVE DEEP VALUES

In everything, the inside is always bigger than the outside. However, there are people who are just a facade, like a house that was left unfinished due to lack of money. They present the entrance to a palace, but the rooms are as poor as those of a hut. There is no place to rest, or maybe they are always resting, because once the greetings are over, the conversation ends. They boast during the initial courtesies, but immediately dive into silence. Words die when they are not fueled by a constant source of intelligence. They only easily deceive people who see appearances, but they do not deceive the cunning person who observes the inside and perceives emptiness.

49

BE CRITICAL AND OBSERVE

Man must dominate things, not let them dominate him. Thus, he will explore the greatest depths and dissect the talents of others with perfection. At a simple glance, man must understand and evaluate the essence of the other, possess great power of observation, decipher even what is well hidden. Observe rigorously, reflect thoughtfully, and argue wisely: there is nothing that cannot be discovered, noticed, grasped and understood.

50

DO NOT LOSE RESPECT FOR YOURSELF

Nor be too tolerant with yourself. Make your integrity the rule of your righteousness. Owe more to the severity of your own discernment than to all external precepts. Avoid the unseemly, not out of fear of harsh judgment from others, but out of consistency with your own prudence and awareness. Respect your own honor.

51

KNOW HOW TO CHOOSE

The gift of knowing how to choose is one of the greatest divine gifts. It is necessary to have good taste and discernment: intelligence and ability are not enough. There is no perfection without judgment and selectivity. Two talents are involved: choosing and choosing the best. Many with fertile & astute intelligence, sensible, diligent and well-informed, get lost when they have to choose. They always choose the worst, as if they made a point of making mistakes.

52

KEEP SELF-CONTROL

Wise people must be very careful not to lose control of themselves. This is what true men argue, as it is difficult for elevated spirits to allow themselves to be shaken. Passions are the moods of the soul, any excess affects prudence. If evil comes out of your mouth, your reputation will be in danger. You need to be complete master of yourself and so great that not even the most prosperous or adverse news can disturb you, but rather makes others admire you.

53

DILIGENCE AND INTELLIGENCE

Diligence, or zeal, quickly executes what intelligence carefully planned. Haste is a passion of fools: as they do not notice important details, they act recklessly. Wise people, on the contrary, tend to sin due to slowness, as common sense forces them to reflect. Sometimes, the correctness of a judgement is nullified by the delay in the action. Promptness is the key to success. Those who do not leave anything for the next day do more. A motto to follow is: hurry slowly.

54

DARE WITH CAUTION

Even hares attack a dead lion. It takes courage. If you give in once, you will end up giving in repeatedly. It is necessary to overcome the same difficulty later, so it is better to take precautions. The mind is bolder than the body. It is like a sword: it must remain carefully sheathed, ready to be used, as it is a defense of a person. A weak spirit is more harmful than a weak body: many who possessed praiseworthy qualities ceased to stand out due to the absence of this breath in heart and left an insignificant legacy. Provident nature ingeniously combined the sweetness of honey with the sting of the bee. In the body, there are nerves as well as bones: do not allow the spirit to be just softness.

55

KNOW HOW
TO WAIT

A great heart is more patient and tolerant. Never be hasty or give vent to your emotions; dominate yourself and you will dominate others. Wander through the open spaces of time toward the center of opportunity. The ability to wait tempers decisions and matures thoughts. The crutch of time is mightier than the steel club of Hercules. God himself does not punish with an iron hand, but with the seasons. A wise saying is: "Time and I can face anyone."

Luck rewards those who know how to wait.

56

BE
CREATIVE

Good ideas arise from a fortunate presence of mind, thanks to its vivacity and relaxation. Those who know how to improvise do not go through difficulties or suffer from setbacks. Some think too much and do everything wrong, while others do everything right without thinking. Some people have antiperistasis reservations: they act better in adversity. It is about those who always get it right, even though they do not think straight. If their understanding does not reach something at the moment, they will never reflect on it later. Speed must be praised, as it reveals a prodigious talent: cunning in thought and caution in actions.

57

IT IS SAFER
TO CONSIDER

Do something well, and you will have done it quickly enough. Everything that is done in a hurry is undone just as quickly, but what should last an eternity also takes a long time to be done. Only perfection is noticed, and only success lasts. Deep understanding reaches eternal truths. What is worth a lot requires a lot. The same happens with metals: the most precious of them takes longer to melt and weighs more.

58

KNOW HOW TO DOSE

You should not show the same intelligence to everyone, nor dedicate more effort than is necessary. Do not waste your knowledge or merit. A good fisherman uses only the bait he needs. Do not show off every day, or you will stop surprising. It is always necessary to keep something new in reserve, because those who show a little every day maintain expectations, and no one ever discovers the limits of their talent.

59

FINISH WELL

In the house of luck, when you enter through the door of pleasure, you leave through the door of sorrow, and vice versa. Therefore, pay attention to how you finish things, worry more about the end than the beginning. The fortunate ones often have very favorable beginnings and very tragic ends. What matters is not being applauded when you arrive, which is common, but being missed when you leave. Rare are those that continue to be desired. Rarely luck accompanies someone to the end. Just as it is kind to those who arrive, it is rude to those who leave..

60

COMMON SENSE

Some are born prudent. They come into the world with an advantage: the natural ability of wise people to discern, which is halfway to success. With age and experience, reason matures, and discernment reaches moderation. Such people abhor any type of whim capable of risking prudence, especially in matters of state, in which security is of paramount importance. These deserve to occupy positions in the government, both in command and on councils.

61

BE SUPERIOR IN
WHAT IS BEST

Among the different types of perfection, it is a rarity. There is no hero without some sublime quality; mediocrity never wins praise. Superiority in a relevant endeavor takes us out of anonymity and makes us remarkable. To be superior in a humble occupation is to be something in very little: the more comfort, the less glory. Being exceptional in superior things gives us a lofty character: it cultivates admiration and earns goodwill.

62

HAVE THE BEST ASSISTANTS

Some people consider themselves smart because they have inferior assistants. It is an illusory and dangerous satisfaction, deserving of punishment. An employee's efficiency never depreciates the value of its boss. On the contrary, all credit for success falls to the main figure, as well as criticism in the case of failure. The superiors are the ones who get the fame. It is never said "he had good or bad employees", but "he was a good or bad manager". So, choose your assistants carefully, you are trusting them with your immortal fame.

63

THE PERFECTION OF BEING THE FIRST

It comes double when you are truly superior. If there is equality in other respects, the one who executes the first movement stands out, and many would have become immortal in their activities, if others had not preceded them. The first ones are those who gain fame, and those who follow them have to claim their daily bread in court. No matter how hard they try, they cannot escape the accusation of being imitators. It is the subtlety of the prodigious to invent new ways to achieve perfection, as long as prudence guarantees the safety of their adventures. Through innovation, wise men find a place on the list of heroes. Some prefer to be first in second class rather than second in first.

64

AVOID DISAPPOINTMENTS

Avoiding annoyances is a sensible and beneficial attitude. Prudence will spare you from many: it is about Lucina, goddess of light and childbirth, happiness and, therefore, satisfaction. Do not give others bad news unless there is a remedy, and be even more careful not to receive it yourself. Some people only have ears for sweet flattery, others for intrigue, and there are those who cannot live without a daily dose of annoyance, like Mithridates with his poison. It also does not help at all to live by depriving yourself of things or contradicting yourself in order to please other people, even if it is someone you love very much. Never put your happiness at stake just to satisfy someone's wishes. When bringing joy to someone means depriving yourself of something or going against yourself, remember this lesson: it is better for someone else to get hurt now than for you to get hurt later, irreparably.

65

DEVELOP A
REFINED TASTE

Good taste requires care, as well as intellect. Total understanding stimulates appetite and desire and, consequently, makes the gratification of achievement greater. It is possible to evaluate the greatness of someone's talent by its aspirations. Only something great can satisfy a great talent, just as the best dishes are made for the best palates, and the highest matters are for those of high character. Even the bravest people are intimidated by those with refined taste, and the most perfect lose their self-confidence. There are few things of the first magnitude: save your appreciation. Good taste is acquired through contact with others and is inherited through continuity. It is fortunate to be able to associate with someone with perfectly developed taste. However, never declare that something does not please you; it is very foolish, even more so when it is out of affectation than out of true displeasure. Some wish God had created another world and other perfections just to satisfy their extravagant imagination.

66

PAY ATTENTION SO THAT
THINGS GO RIGHT

Some people care more about choosing the right path than achieving their goals. The discredit of failure weighs more than good intentions. Whoever wins does not need to give any explanations. Most people do not pay attention to the means used to obtain a result, but rather to the results themselves. Our reputation remains intact when we obtain the desired result. A good ending turns everything into gold, no matter how inadequate the means may have been. The rule is to go against the rules if there is no other way to achieve the desired goal.

67

PREFER COMMENDABLE OCCUPATIONS

Most things depend on the satisfaction of others. Recognition feeds and nourishes perfection. Certain occupations enjoy universal acclaim, while others, although more important, are barely noticed. The first ones, because they happen in front of everyone, earn general admiration. The latter are rarer and require more skill, but they do not appear; they are appreciated but not praised. Among princes, the most celebrated are the victorious, which is why the kings of Aragon were so acclaimed: they were magnanimous warriors and conquerors. The important man must give preference to famous occupations, which everyone can see and share, and he will be immortalized by general acclaim.

68

MAKE OTHERS UNDERSTAND

It is better than making them remember, as intelligence is more important than memory. Sometimes it is needed to remember, other times it is needed to advise what is appropriate. There are people who fail to do what is opportune simply because the idea never occurred to them. May friendly advice highlights the advantages. One of the greatest privileges of the mind is knowing how to quickly evaluate what really matters. Without this discernment, many successes are not realized. Those who have this light must grant it, and those who do not have it, ask for it, the former with caution, the latter with discretion, only insinuating. This subtlety is particularly useful when the person giving advice has some interest or involvement that could influence in their impartiality. Be explicit only when insinuation is not enough. Having already obtained a no, use the skill to seek a yes. Most of the time, you do not get things because you do not try.

69

DO NOT GIVE IN TO
A VULGAR WHIM

Great men do not give in to fleeting impressions. Part of prudence consists in reflecting upon oneself: knowing disposition and taking precautions, or even deviating to the other extreme to, between art and nature, find the point of balance. To correct yourself, you need to know yourself. There are true monsters of impertinence, always governed by some whim, which influences them perniciously. Affected by this imbalance, they undertake their tasks in a contradictory way. Such excess, in addition to ruining the will, also affects reason, damaging desire and understanding.

70

KNOW HOW
TO SAY NO

It is impossible to grant everything to everyone. Saying no is as important as granting, especially among those who command. What matters is how to do it. Some people's denials are more appreciated than others' granting: an embellished "no" pleases more than a laconic "yes". Many always have a negative on the tip of their tongue and turn everything sour; it is the first thing that comes to mind. Even if they later give in, they will no longer be as worthy of consideration, as they were unpleasant in the beginning. You must deny gently, so that the disappointment is assimilated little by little, and without denying things completely, so that others continue to depend on you. Always leave a glimmer of hope to soften the disappointment of negative. Courtesy compensates for the bad feeling of refusal, and kind words compensate for the emptiness caused by frustration. "No" and "Yes" are quick words to say, but they require prolonged reflection.

71

BE CONSISTENT IN TEMPER AND TASTES

The prudent man is consistent in everything that concerns perfection, which justifies his fame. It changes only when the causes and merits change. With regard to prudence, it is ugly to vary. Some people look different every day: their opinion changes constantly, as well as their will and ability to understand. One day they grant; the other they go back. They damage their own reputation, confusing others.

72

BE DECIDED

An imperfect execution is less harmful than a lack of decision, as the matter deteriorates faster when stagnant than in use. Some people are incapable of making a decision and need a push. Sometimes the cause is not in indecision, since they see clearly enough, but in a lack of initiative. Identifying difficulties may be a skill, but finding a way to avoid them requires an even greater skill. Other people do not let anything get them down and have great power of criticism and decision-making. They were born for important missions, as their ability to understand enlightens them to make the right decisions. They soon find a solution, and their self-confidence grows to solve, with increasing common sense, the next question.

73

BE EVASIVE

It is how cautious people avoid undesirable situations. With an elegant joke they can get out of trouble, with a smile they can get rid of a difficulty. This is how the greatest of captains, Gonzalo de Córdoba, acquired his courage. A cordial way to say "no" consists of changing the subject, and no maneuver is more brilliant than pretending you do not understand.

74

DO NOT BE
INTRACTABLE

The most dangerous beasts live in the most populated places. Being inaccessible is the addiction of those who lack self-knowledge and change their mood depending on the circumstances. It is not by being unpleasant to others that you gain fame. Imagine one of those intractable monsters, always ready to explode for anything and everything: those who live with him or have the misfortune of being his subordinates that approach him as if he was a ferocious animal, frightened and full of caution. There are people who, to reach a high position, submit and please anyone and, when they get there, they take revenge by mistreating everyone. If they achieved an important position, they should be liked and trusted, but their pride and arrogance drive people away. The best punishment is to ignore them. Reserve your wisdom for those who deserve it.

75

CHOOSE A
HEROIC MODEL

More to try to surpass them than to imitate them. There are countless examples of greatness, of men who achieved fame. Each person must choose as a model the one who best stood out in their field. Alexander cried with envy over Achilles' grave, not for the hero who had lost his life, but for himself, who had not achieved the same fame. There is nothing that stimulates ambition more than the clarion call of other people's glory. And everything that can defeat envy ennobles the spirit.

76

KNOW HOW TO DOSE JOKES

Prudence is recognized in seriousness, which is more respected than intelligence. The man who keeps joking has no credibility, he is compared to a liar, who no one can trust. From one we fear cheating, from the other, doubt. One never knows when he is being serious, which is equivalent to being a person without common sense. Everything that is excessive loses its value, is tiring and wears out. Some gain a reputation as witty and lose their reputation as sensible. There are moments for fun, but the rest of the time is for seriousness.

77

BE CAPABLE OF ADAPTING

Being cultured with cults and holy with saints: this is the great art of captivating people, as similarity attracts sympathy. Observe the temper of others and try to adapt to them. Observe the temper of others and try to adapt to them. Respond to seriousness or joviality, subtly transforming yourself. This skill is essential for those who depend on others. It is easier for those who are informed, with broad vision and refined taste.

78

CAUTION FIRST

Precipitation and audacity are characteristics of fools. The very lack of intelligence, which prevents them from foreseeing danger, means that, later on, they do not have the feeling of failure. However, prudence walks with great care; observation and caution precede it, paving the way for it to advance safely. A hasty action is doomed to failure, only luck can save it. Move forward slowly when you suspect the terrain is treacherous. Cunning studies the terrain, and prudence leads to solid ground. Nowadays, there are many surprises in human relationships, so it is advisable to explore the path carefully.

79

YOUTHFUL TEMPER

With moderation is a quality, not a defect. A pinch of humor is a good seasoning. Men who stand out gain general sympathy with humor and joviality, without ever leaving aside prudence and decorum. Sometimes a relaxed attitude can help get rid of an embarrassment, as it is necessary to take certain things as a joke, even those that others would take more seriously. This type of temper is more friendly and captivating.

80

PAY ATTENTION WHEN INFORMING YOURSELF

We spend a good part of our lives receiving information, most of what we learn is transmitted to us by someone, not seen or experienced directly. The ears are the back door to truth and the front door to lies. It is easier to see than to hear the truth: it rarely comes to us pure, much less when it comes from far away. Along the way, it acquires colors, reflexes and distortions, which may be favorable or not, depending on the moods and passions of its transmitters, who always try to impress. Pay close attention to those who praise and even more to those who criticize: you need to discover the intentions of the intermediate, know their interests, tendencies and weaknesses. Caution must act as a counterbalance to detect what is false and what is being omitted.

81

RENEW THE BRIGHTNESS

It is a privilege of the phoenix. Perfection ages, as well as fame. Habit wears away admiration, and a mediocre novelty is capable of defeating the greatest celebrity. Therefore, it is necessary to constantly renew intelligence, courage, performance, all qualities, dawning as often as the sun, casting its shine in different and varied directions so that it is missed, awakening desire and applause.

82

NEVER EXAGGERATE

A certain wise man reduced wisdom to moderation in everything. What is right, taken to the extreme, can generate injustice, just as an orange squeezed to the maximum becomes bitter. Even in pleasure we should not exaggerate. Talent itself is exhausted if it is demanded too much, and it takes blood instead of milk, those who suck with excessive voracity.

83

ALLOW YOURSELF SMALL SLIPS

Sometimes a reckless attitude can be the best way to highlight your qualities. Envy dooms everything that is good, it accuses what is perfect of never failing, at the same time it tries to find some flaw, just to console itself. Like lightning, censorship always hits the highest points. So may Homer distract himself from time to time and pretend that his intelligence or courage – but not his prudence – failed somehow. This appeases malevolence, preventing it from discharging its poison. It is like spreading the cape before the bull of envy in order to preserve immortality.

84

KNOW HOW TO USE ENEMIES

Never hold a knife by the blade to avoid injury, but by the handle to defend yourself, especially in competitions. Wise people see more use in their enemies than fools see in their friends. Malevolence is capable of removing mountains of difficulties when it intends to act for its own benefit. Many owe their greatness to their enemies. Flattery is more threatening than resentment, because resentment highlights the defects that flattery disguises. The prudent man uses the hatred of his enemies as a more reliable mirror than that of affection, as it helps him to reduce defects or correct them. One must be very cautious when one lives surrounded by flattery and malevolence.

85

DO NOT BE THE JOKER

Perfect things are easily abused. Greed arouses resentment. It is bad not to be good at anything, but it is even worse to be good at everything. Some lose because they win too often and soon find themselves as despised as they were once admired. There are jokers in all types of perfection, who, when they lose their initial reputation as unique, are scorned as common. The only remedy against exaggeration is to be moderate when revealing your talents: exceed yourself in perfection, but moderate yourself when displaying it. The brighter the torch, the faster it is consumed and the shorter it lasts, while discretion is rewarded with great admiration.

86

GET AWAY
FROM RUMORS

The crowd is a monster with many heads: many eyes for malice, many tongues for slander. Sometimes a rumor that spreads can ruin the best of reputations, forever tarnish a good name. Typically, rumors arise from some salient flaw or ridiculous defect: perfect material for gossip. Sometimes it is envious people who invent such defects, despicable people who, with a sharp tongue, ruin an irreproachable reputation with a malicious comment disguised as a joke, faster than with a blatant lie. It is very easy to lose a good reputation - because it is easy to believe in evil; it is hard to get it back. Cautious people should avoid all this and be attentive for vulgar insolence, as it is easier to be safe than sorry.

87

CULTURE AND
REFINEMENT

Man is born wild; the beast is tamed by cultivating it. Culture transforms us into people: the more so the greater the culture. With this belief, Greece was able to call the rest of the world barbarians. Ignorance is rude and gross, there is nothing more educating than knowledge. However, knowledge itself, without refinement, is crude. It is not only intelligence that we must improve, but also our desires and, mainly, our conversation. Some exhibit a natural refinement in inner and outer talents, in concepts and words, in bodily adornment (which is like the bark) and in spiritual gifts (the fruit). Others are so crude that they blur everything, even their superior qualities, with an unbearable and savage lack of refinement.

88

GREAT MANNERS

Aspire elevation. Great men should never have despicable attitudes. There is no need to address every detail when talking to others, especially when the topic is unpleasant. Observe things in a relaxed way, it is not good to turn the conversation into a detailed interrogation. Act normally with nobility, a type of gallantry. A good part of power is in dissimulation: learn to turn a blind eye to most of what happens between friends, acquaintances and, especially, enemies. Everything that is exaggerated is irritating and, depending on the condition, tiring. Surrounding yourself with something unpleasant is a type of mania. In general, the same happens with the way of behaving, which varies according to the heart and ability of each person.

89

UNDERSTANDING OF YOURSELF

Character, qualities, capacity for discernment and emotional balance. No one can be master of themselves if they do not know themself completely. There are mirrors for the face, but not for the spirit; do then a thoughtful self-reflection. And, when you stop worrying about your outer image, try to correct and improve your inner one. Know the strength of your prudence and perspicacity.

90

THE ART OF LIVING LONG

It is living well. Two things waste life: foolishness and addiction. Some lose it because they do not know how to save it; others, because they do not want to know. Just as virtue is its own reward, addiction is its own punishment. The one who gives themself over to a life of vicissitudes – of imbalance – ends twice as quickly, while the one who gives themself over to virtue never dies. The strength of the mind communicates with the body. A good life is not only great in duration, but also in quality.

91

NEVER ACT WITH DOUBTS

If whoever acts suspects that they may be making a mistake, whoever observes will be absolutely sure of this, especially in the case of a rival. If your common sense fails in the heat of emotion, it will not fail to condemn, later, the mistake made. It is dangerous to undertake something without certainty, it is safer to omit it. Prudence refuses to negotiate with probabilities: it always walks in the light of reason. How can something end well if there were doubts at the beginning? If even unanimously approved decisions can often turn out to be inadequate, what can we expect from those on which reason and common sense had doubts?

92

TRANSCENDENT PRUDENCE

It must be used in all situations. This is the first and most important rule when acting and talking, the more necessary, the bigger and higher the occupation. An ounce of prudence is worth more than a pound of skill. It is better to walk confidently than to court vulgar applause. A reputation earned by prudence constitutes the ultimate triumph of fame. It will be enough to satisfy the prudent ones, whose approval is the door to success.

93

A COMPLETE MAN

A man with many qualities is worth many people. He has joy in life and transmits this joy to those he interacts with. Variety and perfection make life enjoyable. It is a great art to know how to appreciate all good things. Considering that nature made man its masterpiece, may art make him a universe of good taste and intelligence.

94

INSCRUTABLE GIFTS

The prudent man, if he wants to be respected by others, must avoid having them evaluate the extent of his wisdom and his qualities. Allow yourself to be known, but not understood. Do not show the limits of your talent, and no one will be disappointed. Never allow anyone to know you completely: we obtain greater admiration by making others imagine the extent of our talent, or even by doubting it, than by showing it off, however great it may be.

95

KNOW HOW TO KEEP EXPECTATION

Feed it constantly, promise and fulfill, more and more. A remarkable deed generates the expectation of even greater ones. Do not reveal everything you have in the first move: the secret is to moderate your strength and knowledge and, little by little, increase your performance.

96

COMMON SENSE AND DISCERNMENT

They are the cores of reason, the basis of prudence, the light of wisdom. They are gifts from heaven, the most important and precious, and without them, we are incomplete. The fewer they are present, the more they are missed. All acts of life depend on their influence, and all ask for their approval, as they depend on intelligence. It consists of a natural inclination towards everything that is most sensible.

97

BUILD A REPUTATION AND PRESERVE IT

It is the enjoyment of fame. It is expensive, because it is born from superiority, which is as rare as mediocrity is common. Once achieved, it is easily preserved. It requires a lot and produces more. It constitutes a kind of majesty, when it transforms into admiration, for the greatness of its cause and sphere of action. A solid reputation is the one that always has value.

98

DO NOT OPENLY DECLARE YOUR INTENTIONS

Passions are the portals of the soul. The most practical type of knowledge is in dissimulation: the one who shows his cards risks losing. May caution and reservation overcome the opponent's attention. If they try to guess your reasoning, hide your thoughts. Let no one discover your predilections, so that they do not predict them, neither to criticize nor to flatter them.

99

REALITY AND APPEARANCE

We do not define things by what they are, but by what they seem. Rare are those who see the inside, and many who are attached to appearances. It is not enough to just be right; it is necessary that the appearance also demonstrates it.

100

BE REALISTIC WITHOUT SHOWING OFF

Philosophy is no longer revered, although this is still the main occupation of wise men. The science of wisdom is no longer venerated. Seneca, Roman philosopher, writer and politician, introduced it to Rome and for a time it excited the nobles, but now it is considered useless and inopportune. Not being carried away by illusions was always a step towards wisdom and one of the pleasures of rectitude of character.

101

HALF THE WORLD LAUGHS AT THE OTHER HALF

Either everything is good, or everything is bad, depending on the point of view. Those who have followers also have pursuers. It is an incurable fool the one who evaluates everything according to their own opinion, because perfections do not depend on a single taste: they are as abundant as physiognomies, and equally varied. There is no defect that someone will not value, nor should one be discouraged if something did not please some, as there will be no shortage of others who will appreciate it. In the same way, the applause should not flatter, because there will be those who will boo. The rule of true satisfaction consists of receiving approval from people with reputation, honesty and credibility. Life is not governed by a single opinion.

102

VALUE YOUR LUCK

Wisdom has recognition and moderation. The body of wisdom must have a huge stomach, as a large capacity depends on appropriate space.

Some waste fine foods because they do not know how to enjoy it. They were not born for high occupations and are not accustomed to them. The coexistence is ruined and the vanity that emanates from undeserved honor goes to the head, affecting reason. They inflate until they no longer fit within themselves, until there is no more room for their own luck and prosperity. The remarkable man knows and shows that he still has room for better things and, cautiously, avoids everything that reveals a petty heart.

103

MAJESTY THAT FITS EACH ONE

Not everyone is a king, but their actions must be worthy of one, within the limits of their class and condition. A royal way of doing things is to have greatness of action and a sublime mind. It is necessary to resemble a king in merit, even if you are not, because true sovereignty lies in integrity. We will not envy greatness if we ourselves are a standard of it. Those who find themselves close to the throne, in particular, must contract some of the true superiority. They must share the moral gifts of majesty rather than those of pomp, and aspire to high and substantial things rather than imperfect vanity.

104

HAVE A GOOD SENSE OF THE REQUIREMENTS OF EACH JOB

Understanding the varieties of occupations requires knowledge and perspicacity. Some jobs require courage, others require subtlety. The easiest ones depend on honesty, the hardest ones require cunning. The first ones require only natural talent, the latter, all types of attention and vigilance. It is difficult to govern men, even more those who are foolish or crazy, as it is necessary to have doubled intelligence to control those who have none. A job that requires absolute dedication, with fixed and routine hours, is unbearable. Much better are those that do not leave us bored, in which variety is combined with responsibility, because breaking routine revives us. The best occupations are those that allow flexibility and independence, the worst ones are those that distance us from the human condition and, worse, from the divine condition.

105

DO NOT BE BORING

A person who has only one subject, one obsession, becomes boring. It is more productive and pleasant to be brief and practical: what is lost in brevity is gained in courtesy. Good things, if they are brief, become even better. The bad ones, when they are brief, stop being so unpleasant. It is more productive to say what is essential than to go into endless details. Everyone knows that a very talkative person is rarely understood, not necessarily in the subject, but in the speech as a whole. There are men whose conversation generates more embarrassment than joy and they are always avoided. A discreet man avoids annoying others, especially important people, who are always very busy. Annoying one of them is worse than annoying the rest of the world. The best way to say something well is to say it briefly and outright.

106

DO NOT BRAG

It is more reprehensible the one who brags of his high position. Do not brag, for this is detestable, and do not be proud of being envied. The more you try to earn the esteem of others, the less you will achieve, as it is not something that can be taken by force, you have to deserve it and wait for it. Important occupations require the corresponding authority, without which it will not be possible to exercise them properly. Perform only what your occupation requires to fulfill obligations. Do not exhaust it; help it to move forward. Those who really want to appear extremely dedicated to their work give the impression that they are not up to the task. If you want to stand out, use talent, not appearances. Even a king must be venerated more for his intrinsic sovereignty than for that which was inherited or conferred.

107

DO NOT SHOW TOO MUCH SATISFACTION

Do not live eternally discontented with yourself, which is pettiness, nor eternally satisfied, which is foolishness. Self-satisfaction typically originates from ignorance and leads to foolish happiness, which provides pleasure and harms reputation. Those who cannot evaluate the perfection of others are content with their own mediocrity. Caution is always useful, whether to obtain good results or to console ourselves when they are not exactly what we expected. No adversity will surprise those who have already prepared themselves in advance. It all depends on the circumstances; what is positive in one situation may be negative in another. The fool's mistake is to let that satisfaction blossom empty and scatter its seeds.

108

SHORTCUT TO BE A VALUEABLE PERSON

It is very useful to associate with the right people. Coexistence can bring about wonderful transformations: habits, tastes and even intelligence are transmitted in this way without one realizing it. Therefore, the person who is insecure should seek the company of those who are decisive and self-confident, and so on. This way, they will achieve balance and moderation. However, it takes skill to adapt. The alternation of opposites makes the universe beautiful and balances it, and in human relationships it promotes even greater harmony than in nature. Remember this when choosing friends and employees; communicating extremes will produce a discreet and valuable compromise.

109

DO NOT CENSOR OTHERS

There are ruthless men who make everything a crime, not out of passion, but due to their own temper. They condemn everyone, some for what they did, others for what they will do. These are spirits that are more than cruel, they are truly petty. They criticize others with such exaggeration that they turn a speck into a reason to pull out their eyes. They are like taskmasters, who can turn a paradise into hell. When dominated by passion, they take everything to extremes. Naivety, on the contrary, creates excuses for everything, insists on saying that others had good intentions or made inadvertent mistakes.

110

DO NOT WAIT FOR THE SUN TO SET

The sensible person prefers to withdraw before finding itself abandoned. We must make even our own death a triumph. Sometimes the sun itself hides behind a cloud, so that no one sees it set, making us wonder if it has already set or not. Avoid declines to avoid falling and breaking down: do not wait for people to turn their back on you, as it is like being buried alive and dying to fame. Cautious people know when to retire a racehorse, they do not expect it to suffer a fall during a competition and arouse criticism and censure.

111

MAKE FRIENDS

The friend is a second being. For him, all friends are good and wise. When you are with them, everything ends well. You are worth as much as others think or say you are and, for them to want you, you must gain them through your heart. Nothing fascinates more than a good service, and the best way to gain friends is to act like one. The most and best we are, depends on others. We can live among friends or enemies: find a friend every day, even if not close. Choose well and some will become confidants.

112

EARN THE GOOD WILL OF OTHERS

Reputation is earned with affection. Some are so confident in their own value that they do not worry about it, but the one who is prudent knows very well that a favor can open a shortcut to merits and qualities. Benevolence makes everything easier and makes up for whatever is lacking: courage, integrity, wisdom, even discretion. It never sees the ugliness, because it does not want to see it. Typically, it originates from affinities of temper, race, family, nationality or profession. In the spiritual sphere, benevolence confers talent, esteem, reputation and merit. Once conquered, which is difficult, it is easy to preserve it. The important thing is to know how to use it.

113

GET READY FOR DIFFICULTIES

Supply for the winter takes place calmly in the summer. In times of abundance and prosperity, favors are less expensive, and friendships are many. It is good to save for bad times, when adversity is costly, and everything is lacking. Keep a reserve of friends and grateful people; someday you will value what now seems unimportant. Pettiness has no friends in prosperity, because it refuses to recognize them, nor in adversity, when they are the ones who refuse.

114

NO COMPETITION

If we compete with our opponents, our reputation can be damaged, as the rival will immediately try to discover our defects and discredit us. There are few who act within the precepts of honesty and justice. Rivalry discovers faults that courtesy had forgotten. Many had a good reputation until they made enemies. The heat of the dispute awakens dormant infamies and unearths past and previous sordidness. In competition, defects reveal themselves and rivals take advantage of everything they can and should not. They gain nothing by offending others, only the petty pleasure of revenge. It strikes such violent blows that it shakes off the dust of oblivion that covered its defects. Benevolence was always peaceful, and reputation, indulgent.

115

TOLERATE THE DEFECTS OF OTHERS

Just like with ugly faces, we should ignore bad moods of other people. Where there is dependence, aspire to convenience. There are minds so evil that you cannot live with them, even though we often have no choice. It takes skill to get used to them. At first they frighten us, but, little by little, that initial aversion is lost, and caution stops being surprised and learns to tolerate displeasure.

116

JOIN GOOD PEOPLE

It is possible to commit to them and accept their commitments. Good character guarantees that they will treat you well even when they oppose you, as they behave correctly. It is better to have a disagreement with a good person than to subjugate a characterless person.

There is no way to have a good relationship with villainy, as it does not respect the commitment to loyalty and honor. Be wary of their pleasantries, as these people do not know what integrity is. There is no true friendship between petty people. Avoid them, because those who do not value honor do not appreciate virtue. And honor is the cradle of integrity.

117

DO NOT TALK ABOUT YOURSELF

Neither to praise yourself, which is vanity, nor to criticize yourself, which is humility. Either one is boring to the listener. And if this is important among friends, it is even more in high positions. When speaking in public frequently, any display of vanity is counterproductive. It is also not advisable to talk about people who are present, as you risk exaggerating flattery or saying slander.

118

GAIN FAME AS CORDIAL

Cordiality is the most important thing in any relationship; it enchants, captivates and earns everyone's good will, just as rudeness only earns contempt and ill will. When it results from pride, rudeness is detestable; when it refers to lack of manners, it is despicable. Excessive cordiality is preferable to lack of it; and cordiality should not be equal to everyone, as it would be unfair. Among enemies, cordiality is a duty, as it shows that you are a worthy opponent. It costs little and brings great benefits, because those who respect are respected. Kindness and respect have the advantage of being perpetuated: one in those who use it, and the other in those who gain it.

119

DO NOT BE DISLIKED

There is no need to provoke aversion, it comes without being called. There are people who hate without a fair or specific reason, without knowing why. Responsibility prevents malevolence. Irascibility is more effective and quick to destroy than courtesy to build. There are people who manage to cause a bad impression on everyone, because they are unpleasant or have a bad temper. And once aversion takes hold, it is like a bad reputation: difficult to erase. The correct men are respected, the slanderers annoy, the arrogant arouse antipathy, the self-satisfied are abominable and those with outstanding superiority are abandoned. Show your esteem if you want to be liked, and if you want to be rewarded with success, give others your attention.

120

LIVE IN A PRACTICAL WAY

Even knowledge must accompany need, and where it is non- existent, pretend ignorance. Times change, as well as thoughts, ways of expressing oneself and taste. Do not express yourself conservatively and update your tastes and ideas. The taste of the majority generally prevails. One must follow the general taste, while moving towards evolution, accommodating oneself to the present even if the past seems better, both in the adornments of the body and of the soul. Only when it comes to firmness of character this rule does not apply, as virtue must always be practiced. Many things started being considered old-fashioned, such as telling the truth and keeping one's word. Good men seem to belong to the good old times, although they are always loved. If some still exist, they are rare and never imitated. What a sad time this is, when virtue is ridiculed and malice, appreciated! Wise people live the best way they can, even if it is not how they would like. They prefer what luck granted them to what it refused them.

121

AVOID A STORM IN A TEACUP

Some people overlook everything, while others make drama out of anything. They take everything to heart and turn any issue into controversy or fatality. Few problems are really important enough to justify our annoyance. It is foolish to take seriously what we should turn our backs on. Many important things lose their value when neglected, while others, without the slightest importance, increase because we pay attention to them. In the beginning, it is easy to put an end to problems, but later on, it becomes difficult. Sometimes the medicine causes the disease. A good rule of life is to let it go!

122

ELEGANCE IN WORDS AND ACTIONS

Elegance opens all doors and wins respect in advance. It influences everything: the practice of virtues, performance, even walking, looking, wanting. It is a great victory to captivate the hearts of others. Elegance does not arise from foolish audacity or boring fun, but from a superior character enriched by merit.

123

DO NOT BE AFFECTED

The purer the qualities of a person, the less affectation it shows. Affectation is a vulgar defect, as annoying to others as it is uncomfortable for those who show it, as it is a torment to have to keep appearances. The most praiseworthy qualities lose their value because of affectation, because they are attributed to an artifice rather than to a natural talent, and the natural is always more pleasant. Normally, those affected are seen as boasting qualities that they do not possess. The better a person is at something, the more they must try to disguise their efforts, so that perfection seems a natural consequence. To escape affectation, one should not pretend not to have it either. A discreet man should not demonstrate that he is aware of his own merits, as the slightest slip will draw the attention of others to him. Whoever keeps their qualities to themself is twice as superior. Compliments should come from the outside in, not the other way around.

124

MAKE YOURSELF WANTED

Few people gain the sympathy of others, so consider yourself happy if you manage to gain that of the wise ones. The best way to conquer and preserve the great privilege of esteem is to stand out in your qualities and in what you do. Make your qualities become indispensable, so that people say that the occupation needs you, and not the other way around. Some honor their position, others are honored by it. It is no advantage to be considered good just because your successor is bad, as this does not mean that you are actually wanted, but rather that the other is detestable.

125

DO NOT CONTROL
OTHER PEOPLE'S DEFECTS

Paying attention to other people's imperfections reveals that your own fame is ruined. Some like to disguise or justify their own defects by highlighting those of others: this is a consolation for fools. Whoever digs deeper gets dirtier and few escape having some defect, whether by inheritance or by alliance. Only when we are little known that our faults are unknown. Anyone who is sensible should not register other people's defects, so not to become the type of person everyone prefers to avoid.

126

IF YOU DO SOMETHING FOOLISH, DISGUISE IT

Hide your feelings, and even more your flaws. Everyone makes mistakes, but with one difference: wise people disguise their mistakes, while fools announce even those they have yet to make. A good reputation depends more on caution than on fact. If you cannot be chaste, be cautious. The mistakes of great men are more evident, like the eclipses of the Sun and the Moon. We should not confess our defects to our friends or to ourselves, if possible. Another rule of good living applies here: knowing how to forget.

127

NATURALITY AND GRACE

They give life to talent, voice to expression, soul to actions and highlight even the highest gifts. The other qualities constitute an adornment of nature, but natural grace adorns the perfections themselves: it even makes thought more admirable. It owes more to natural talent and less to effort, it is superior even to discipline, faster than mere skill and achieves even what is daring. It increases self-confidence and wisdom. Without it, all beauty is dead, all grace is disgrace. It transcends merit, discretion, prudence and majesty itself. It is a skillful way in business and an elegant way to get rid of any difficulties.

128

GREATNESS OF SOUL

One of the main requirements of heroism, as it inspires all types of greatness. Elevates taste, ennobles the heart, stimulates thought, ennobles character and provides magnificence. It stands out wherever it is. Luck, envious at times, tries to deny it, but it longs to distinguish itself. It governs the will, even when restricted by circumstances. Magnanimity, generosity and all other superior qualities recognize it as their source.

129

NEVER COMPLAIN

Complaints always generate discredit. Instead of arousing people's compassion and comfort, it exalts passion and arrogance, encouraging those who hear our complaints to act like those we complain about. Once disclosed, the offenses done to us seem to make the next ones forgivable. Some complain about past offenses and motivate future ones. They want a remedy or a consolation, but they arouse complacency and even disdain. The best policy is to praise the favors others did you, so as to get even more. By commenting on how those absent favored you, you ask those present to do the same, to pay with the same coin. An attentive man should never disclose discredit or slights, only the appreciation that others have shown him. Thus, he wins friends and reduces enemies.

130

SEEM WHAT YOU ARE

Things are not interpreted for what they are, but for what they seem, and standing out is knowing how to show yourself twice. What cannot be seen is as if it did not exist. Reason itself is not respected when it does not present a reasonable face. The deluded ones are more numerous than the cautious ones, deception prevails, as things are judged from the outside, rarely being what they appear to be. A beautiful exterior is the best way to demonstrate inner perfection.

131

NOBILITY OF CHARACTER

The soul has its fine clothes, they are the spiritual impetus and boldness, which make the heart seem splendid. Not everyone has nobility, as this requires magnanimity. Your first concern is always to speak well of the enemy and act even better. A person with this quality shines more intensely when they have the opportunity to take revenge, as they takes advantage of such situations to transform a potential act of revenge into unexpected generosity. They never show off their triumphs and, when these are due to merit, they know how to dissimulate them.

132

RECONSIDER

Safety lies in analyzing situations twice, especially when you are not completely confident of which path to take. Take your time, whether to fulfill a request or to improve your situation, and you will find new ways to make sure of your choices. A gift is more valued when given wisely than when given hastily, as what is desired for a long time is always more appreciated. When refusing, do it gently and let the "no" mature a little so that it does not turn out to be so bitter. Most of the time, the first heat of desire will have dissipated, and it will be easier to accept the refusal. If someone asks for something quickly, take your time to grant it; it is a way to keep interest.

133

A WISE MAN IS OF NO USE ALONE

That is what politicians say. If everyone is crazy, you will not be criticized, but if you are the only sensible one, you will be considered crazy. The important thing is to go with the flow. Sometimes the greatest wisdom is not knowing or pretending not to know. We have to live with others, and most are ignorant. To live alone, you have to be a little divine or primitive. However, I would moderate this aphorism by saying: better a wise man among many than a madman alone.

134

DOUBLE WHATEVER IS NECESSARY

Doing this is doubling life. Do not depend on one thing, nor limit any resource, no matter how rare and excellent. Double everything, especially the sources of benefit, privilege and good taste. The mutability of the moon is transcendent and establishes the end of permanence. And even more changeable are the things that depend on the fragile human will. Accumulate supplies for times of fragility. It is a great rule of life to double the sources of happiness and profit. Just as nature duplicated the most important and most exposed limbs of the body, art must duplicate the things we depend on.

135

DO NOT BE CONTRARY

So as not to be considered foolish and annoying. Common sense should annihilate this type of behavior. Presenting objections to everything may be original, but the stubborn person is almost always a fool. Some turn pleasant conversations into arguments and are more enemies of those close to them than of those with whom they have no relationship. Just as it is in the tastiest part of the meat that there is more bone, the spirit of contradiction ruins happy moments. Anyone who is contrary to everything, in addition to being unbearable, is a fool.

136

GET TO THE HEART OF THE MATTER

Get to the point. Many create endless discussions, waste their efforts by talking endlessly, arguing uselessly, without getting to the heart of the matter. They go round and round, tiring themselves and others, and never get to what matters. They have a confused mind and do not know how to start. They waste time and patience on what would have been better ignored, and then there is no more time for what they left undone.

137

THE WISE MAN IS ENOUGH FOR HIMSELF

One friend, one universal man, is enough to replace Rome and the rest of the universe. May each one be that friend to themself, and they will be able to live for themself. Who could you miss if no taste and no intellect is superior to yours? It will only depend on yourself, and the greatest happiness is to resemble the Supreme Being. Whoever is able to live for themself will have nothing brute, but much wisdom, and everything of God.

138

DO NOT MEDDLE

Even less in troubled situations. Human relationships have turmoil, storms of will, times when it is wiser to withdraw to a safe haven and let the waves calm down. Medicines often make illnesses worse. In certain cases, nature must be allowed to act, in others, morality must act. An experienced doctor knows when to prescribe a medicine or not, as sometimes the solution is not to give medicine. Every once in a while, shrugging your shoulders is a good way to withstand a storm. If you give time to time, you will achieve victory. If anything clouds the waters of a stream, it is useless to make efforts to clean them; with continuity and rest, they will become crystal clear again. In the midst of the turmoil, any small spark can make the situation even worse. The best medicine is to let the confusion run its course, until it is resolved by itself.

139

SEE WHEN LUCK IS NOT IN YOUR FAVOR

There are days when nothing goes right. Even if you change the game, bad luck will persist. Try your luck a few times and withdraw if you realize that it is not on your side. Even intelligence has its flaws; no one can be wise all the time. All perfection depends on a certain moment; beauty is not always in shape. Discretion belies itself, giving in or exceeding itself. Each thing has its time to come true. There are days when everything goes wrong, no matter how hard you try otherwise, and others when, without the slightest effort, everything goes well; everything is accomplished with ease: the intellect is sharp, the disposition is excellent. Take advantage of these days, do not waste a moment. However, never consider a question definitively good or bad; all things can be the result of good or bad luck.

140

SEE THE GOOD SIDE OF EVERYTHING

That is what those with good taste try to do. The bee goes straight to the sweetness, which leads to the hive; the viper, to the bitterness it needs for its poison. So it is with tastes: some are attracted to the best, others to the worst. There is nothing that does not have something good, especially books, which are a product of thought. Some people have such a petty character that, among a thousand qualities and perfections, they find the only defect, which they criticize and increase. They collect weaknesses and failures of will and intelligence, and burden themselves with infamies and defects, not because they are perceptive, but rather as a punishment for their lack of discernment. They are unhappy, because they revel with imperfections and feed on bitterness. The happiest is the person who, among a thousand defects, notices at least one quality.

141

DO NOT LISTEN TO YOURSELF

There is no point in pleasing yourself if you do not please others, as presumption only generates contempt. When you give yourself credit, you accumulate debts towards others. It is impossible to talk and listen to yourself: talking to yourself may be considered crazy, but liking to listen to yourself in front of others is even crazier. There are people who repeatedly use expressions such as: "Right"?, "Isn't it"?, "Do you understand"?, tiring listeners in search of approval or flattery and revealing doubt about their own opinion. The proud ones also like to have an echo when they speak, their conversation is extremely arrogant, always requiring the futile and foolish "Very well, I agree"!

142

DO NOT DEFEND THE WRONG SIDE

Just because the opponent stepped forward and chose the best. It is a battle already lost, good will never be supplanted by evil. If your opponent was smart enough to realize what was right, it would be foolish of you to defend what is wrong. Those who are obstinate in their actions take more risks than those who are stubborn in their words, as it is always riskier to do than to speak. The ignorance of the stubborn ones prevents them from seeing the truth and practicality, for them it is more important to oppose and compete. Prudent people are on the side of reason, not passion, either because they took precautions or because they corrected themselves in time. If the opponent is a fool, the desire to counter will make them follow the opposite path to theirs, even if it is the wrong path. Therefore, to get them out of the way, the only solution is to join them: their own foolishness and stubbornness will make them change sides and annihilate them.

143

AVOID PARADOX JUST TO NOT BE VULGAR

Neither extreme generates credibility, as anything that threatens dignity is senseless. Eccentricity may, at first, seem attractive and surprising with its novelty. However, later, when it reveals its falsehood, it collapses. It has a kind of false enchantment, which in politics can ruin a nation. Those who cannot distinguish themselves through virtue adopt eccentricity, surprising fools and turning wise men into prophets. Eccentricity reveals a lack of discernment and prudence, it is based on falsehood or uncertainty and puts dignity at risk.

144

GRANT TO WIN

A strategy to get what you want, used even by saints to solve problems in heaven. This is a type of dissimulation, useful for gaining allies and the goodwill of others. You demonstrate that you have the same interests as the other person, only to pave the way for yours. Never treat issues in a confusing way, especially risky ones. Beware of those whose first word is usually "no". The best thing is to disguise your intention as much as possible, especially if you sense resistance from the other side or, even worse, aversion. It is a trick for those who act with second intentions, which requires great cunning.

145

DO NOT SHOW YOUR WEAK POINT

If you do not protect an injured finger, everything will hit it. Never complain about your failure, because other people's evil always targets what hurts or weakens us. Show yourself vulnerable and you will only encourage others to take advantage of it. Malevolence is always alert, looking for ways to play its tricks; it uses insinuation to find out where it hurts and knows a thousand stratagems to poke the wounds. Therefore, be cautious and do not expose your weak points, both personal and inherited, as even luck sometimes likes to hit where it hurts. Do not reveal what ails you or what cheers you up, so that the first one does not last, and the latter does not end.

146

SEE DEEP INSIDE

Things are rarely what they seem. Ignorance – which sees nothing beyond the external appearance – often becomes disillusioned when it penetrates the interior of things. In everything, the lie arrives first, dragging a legion of fools behind it. The truth is always late, it is always the last to arrive, limping against time. The cautious ones always reserve one ear for the truth, thanking nature for having given them two. The superficial deceives the unwary; the truth lives more hidden, to be more appreciated by the wise ones.

147

BE ACCESSIBLE

No one is perfect enough to never need advice. The one who refuses to listen is an incorrigible fool. Even the most independent man must accept advice from friends, and even superiors can learn from subordinates. Some people are incorrigible because they are inaccessible, and they fall because no one dares to support them. Even the most inflexible people should leave the door open for friendship, as help can come through it. Everyone needs a friend who feels free to scold and advise. Trust – reinforced by loyalty and prudence – grants this authority. We should not give our respect and trust to anyone, but, without leaving aside caution, we need a faithful confidant, who is like a mirror for us, which shows us right and wrong.

148

THE ART OF CONVERSATION

It is essential for a true person. No human activity demands more attention because none is more common. It is through it that we lose or win. It is necessary to have prudence when writing a letter, which is a thought and written conversation, and even more when speaking, as discretion is soon put to the test. Words are the reflection of the soul. To be successful in a conversation, you need to adapt to the interlocutor's temper and intelligence. Do not correct other people's words, much less their opinions, as this will make people avoid you, preventing you from communicating. In conversation, discretion is more important than eloquence.

149

LET ANOTHER PERSON TAKE THE BLOW

You will protect yourself from malevolence. It is a policy adopted by those who govern; making someone else take the blame for failure and being the target of criticism is not a fault, but a superior skill. Not everyone can do well, and it is not possible to please everyone. So, look for a scapegoat, someone who is a good target due to their own ambition.

150

KNOW HOW TO SELL YOUR PRODUCT

It is not enough to have intrinsic value, as not everyone has the ability to grasp the essentials: the majority follow the crowd – they go because they see other people going. It takes a lot of skill to explain the true value of something. You can use praise, as praise arouses desire, or you can give things a good name, being careful not to use affectation. Another secret is to offer something only to the wise ones, since everyone thinks they are one and those who are not, want to be one. Never praise something for being easy or common: it will make it seem vulgar and worthless. Everyone seeks something unique; uniqueness pleases both the taste and the intellect.

151

THINK WITH ANTICIPATION

First of all, plan for tomorrow. This is the most important of foresight. Those who take precautions do not get into trouble and are better able to face setbacks. Think about how to resolve difficult situations and use reasoning to prevent and avoid them. It is better to sleep with worry than to lose sleep because of it. There are people who act before thinking, then look for excuses instead of consequences. Other people do not think before or after. Throughout life, one must think about the next step to set the course, as precaution and foresight are very useful instruments for living in anticipation.

152

RUN AWAY FROM THE COMPANY OF NEGATIVE PEOPLE

It does not matter if they are considered superior or inferior. The one who exceeds in perfection surpasses in recognition. The other person will always play the main role, and you the secondary one; if you get any respect, it will be just leftovers. When it is alone in the sky, the Moon competes only with the stars, but as soon as the Sun appears it disappears or, if it remains, its brightness loses its strength. Avoid approaching people who could dim your brightness, only allow those who enhance it. Do not have a nuisance by your side, nor exalt others to the detriment of your own reputation. To grow, follow your superiors. After growing, follow the average ones.

153

AVOID FILLING THE GAP
LEFT BY SOMEONE

If you do, try to make sure you meet all the conditions to be successful. Remember that to match your predecessor, you have to be worth twice as much. Just as it takes cunning to stand out from your successor, it needs perspicacity to stand up to those who came before. Filling an important position is difficult, because the past always seems better. It is not enough to match the previous one; the first ones always have an advantage. You need to go further, have a skill that surpasses your predecessor in reputation.

154

DO NOT RUSH TO
BELIEVE OR TO ACT

We know a person's maturity by how long it takes to believe. Lying is common, while credibility must be extraordinary. Hasty conclusions cause conflicts. Another thing: do not openly doubt the honesty of others. Treating someone as a liar, or claiming that they deceived, would be inelegant and insulting. Furthermore, doubting others implies that we ourselves are unworthy of belief. The liar suffers twice, because they neither believe nor are believed. Sensible people think a lot before acting. There are people who lie with words, but also with attitudes, which is worse.

155

DOMINATE YOUR PASSIONS

From time to time, stop and reflect. This avoids impulse actions. Sensible people act with moderation. The first step is to be aware that you are being moved by emotions and know your limits, to have control over your feelings and know when to stop. Through reasoning, move in and out of anger. Try to control yourself, as the hardest thing about running is stopping. It is a great demonstration of superiority to remain calm in conflicting moments. Excessive passion clouds reason. Now with caution, anger will never override common sense. Passion is like a horse galloping unbridled and caution is the reins.

156

SELECT YOUR FRIENDSHIPS

Try to analyze friendships through discretion and understanding. Most friendships are born out of mere chance. We are judged by the friends we have, and wise people never get along with fools. Enjoying someone's company does not make them a close friend. Sometimes we appreciate their sense of humor without fully trusting their talent. Some friendships are legitimate, others are adulterous. The latter are for pleasure, the former are fertile and promote success. The perception of a friend is worth more than the good will of many others, so it is better for your choices to be the dominant factor, not chance. Sensible friends keep problems away, while fools accumulate them. Few have friendships for people, many for fortune.

157

DO NOT DELUDE YOURSELF WITH PEOPLE

It is the worst and most common way to be deceived. It is better to be cheated on the price than on the merchandise. There is nothing that requires more deep and careful evaluation than the human soul. There is a big difference between understanding things and knowing people. It is a great art to understand personality and distinguish between different types of temper. Human nature must be studied as equally as books.

158

ENJOY THE BEST
OF FRIENDSHIPS

Healthy relationships require common sense, skill and discretion. Some people are ideal to keep close, others are more beneficial when they are far away. Those who are not good at talking may be good at exchanging letters. Distance alleviates certain defects that, in proximity, can be unbearable. One should not only seek pleasure in company, but also benefit. A friend is everything, and friendship presents the three qualities of good: unity, kindness and truth. There are few people who can be intimate, and when we do not know how to choose, they become even more rarefied. Knowing how to maintain a friendship is more important than gaining a new one. Look for lasting ones and understand that a new friend could one day be an old friend, and the best are the ones in which we invest the most time. Life without friends is emptier than a desert. Friendship multiplies good and divides evil. It is the only medicine against adversity and food for the soul.

159

KNOW HOW TO
TOLERATE FOOLS

The wise people are less tolerant, because knowledge always demands more. They have less patience. Broad knowledge is hard to please. Epictetus says that the most important rule of life is knowing how to bear all things: with these words he defined half of wisdom. To tolerate all foolishness, it takes a lot of patience. Sometimes we tolerate more from those we depend on most, which helps us overcome ourselves. Patience brings us an invaluable inner peace, which is earthly happiness. Those who do not know how to tolerate others must take refuge in themselves, if they are capable of tolerating themselves.

160

SPEAK PRUDENTLY

Be careful with your opponents and be worthy with everyone else. There is always time to say a word, but never to erase what was said. Speak as if you were writing a will: the fewer words, the fewer lawsuits. Train on unimportant things to learn the most important ones. Restraint and discretion always have a greater attraction. The one who speaks lightly and about everything risks being defeated and appearing cocky.

161

KNOW YOUR OWN DEFECTS

Any person, even the most evolved, is not free of flaws. The problem is in accommodating to them or even reinforcing them. There are defects of the intellect, which are greater, or more easily noticed, in very intelligent people. Generally, they cultivate and love their flaws. Two evils in one: irrational love for addiction. They are like blemishes on a perfect face: they bother others, but to us they seem like charming details. The man who wants to improve himself needs to strive to overcome himself and further improve his qualities, as a defect is more quickly noticed than any quality. Instead of admiring the good things we have, they emphasize the bad ones. Therefore, our positive gifts are devalued.

162

OVERCOME ENVY AND EVIL

Envy should be despised, but kindness is worth much more than indifference. There is nothing more praiseworthy than speaking well of someone who speaks ill of us and there is no nobler revenge than overcoming envy with merit and talent. Each of our successes is torture for those who wish us unhappiness, and our glory is hell for our adversaries. It is the greatest of punishments: turning our happiness into poison for those who wish us evil. The envious person does not die just once, but as many times as their rival is applauded. One's lasting fame is an eternal punishment for their enemies. The first one lives forever with their glories, the last one with their suffering. The trumpets of fame sound to announce the immortality of one and the death of others, condemning them to the scaffold of their own pettiness.

163

DO NOT BECOME UNHAPPY OUT OF COMPASSION

What one considers misfortune, the other considers luck. There is no happy person without many being unhappy. It is common for the unfortunate to gain the compassion of others, so that they want to compensate them with a useless privilege, to the insult of luck. The one who was hated by everyone in prosperity suddenly gains general piety. Their fall turns revenge into compassion. It is necessary to observe how luck deals the cards. There are people who only connect with those who are unhappy. They stop next to the unfortunate person they previously avoided. Sometimes this attitude reveals inner nobility, but it is just a lack of perspicacity.

164

LEAVE SOME THINGS IN EXPECTATION

To test acceptance and receptivity, especially when there is doubt about the pleasing or success. This makes it possible to study whether an undertaking has a chance of being successful and allows you to decide whether to proceed or retreat. When probing the will of others, the sensible person knows where they step. Precaution is essential when asking, wanting and acting.

165

PLAY FAIR

A wise man can fight, but not with baseness. Each person must act according to their convictions, and not as others say they should. Behaving with decency and dignity in a competition is a praiseworthy attitude. Fight not only to acquire power, but also to show superior manners. Winning with disloyalty is not victory, it is surrender, and generosity is always superior. A man of integrity does not use prohibited weapons, even when a friendship ends in resentment. Do not destroy the trust they once placed in you, as anything that insinuates disloyalty contaminates your reputation. In good men, any unworthy attitude causes strangeness. In noble nature, there is no place for villainy and pettiness. The man of integrity must be proud that honesty, generosity and loyalty, although rare, are part of his character.

166

DISTINGUISH THE MAN OF WORDS FROM THE MAN OF ACTIONS

The distinction is subtle, but necessary. It is like the one between the friend who values us for who we are and the one who values us for what we have. Evil words, even without evil actions, are harmful. It is worse to say good words and commit bad actions. No one lives on words, which are like wind, nor on courtesy, which can be artificial. The mirror is the perfect trap to catch birds: only futile people are satisfied with wind. To have value, words must be backed by actions. Trees that do not bear fruit, only leaves, generally do not have hearts. You need to know how to differentiate fruit trees from those that only provide shade.

167

BE SELF-CONFIDENT

In difficult situations, the best ally is to have a strong heart. People who have confidence in themselves face adversity better, as bad times are less desperate for those who know their worth. Do not give in to misfortune, as it will become even more unbearable. There are people who intensify suffering because they do not know how to deal with it. The one who knows themself overcomes their weakness with reflection, and the sensible ones can overcome everything, even the stars.

168

DO NOT BECOME A MONSTER OF NONSENSE

The world is full of futile, presumptuous, stubborn, eccentric, convinced, extravagant, paradoxical, frivolous, gossipy and undisciplined people. They are all monsters of impertinence. Spiritual monstrosity is more serious than bodily monstrosity, because it contradicts superior beauty. However, who will correct all this levity? Where righteousness is lacking there is no place for advice and guidance, as the richness of the spirit is set aside by an ill-conceived desire for imaginary applause.

169

IT IS BETTER TO NOT DO SOMETHING WRONG EVEN ONCE THAN TO DO SOMETHING RIGHT A HUNDRED TIMES

No one looks directly at the shining sun, but everyone does so when an eclipse occurs. Many successes do not attract as much general attention as a single failure. The wicked ones are better known for criticism than the good ones for praise. Many men became popular after doing something wrong or reprehensible, and all their successes are insufficient to cover up a single slip-up. Be sure that malevolence will notice all your defects and none of your virtues.

170

HAVE RESERVES IN ALL THINGS

Do not waste talents or spend all your strength in any situation. Even in knowledge, retain one part: you will double your perfections. It is necessary to always have a reserve for emergency situations, as a timely rescue is more valued and respected than an impertinent attack. Prudence always follows a safe path and, in this sense, it is easy to understand the strange paradox: half is more than the whole.

171

DO NOT WASTE FAVORS

Keep useful friends for possible difficult occasions. Do not waste your good graces or use your contacts for matters of little importance. Save your trump cards until they are really needed. If you exchange a lot for a little, what will be left for later? There is nothing more valuable than being able to benefit from someone, nor anything more precious than favor: it makes or destroys anything, and can even grant a talent or take it away. The wise ones, the more favored by Nature and fame, the more envied by luck. It is better to preserve and count on the help of people than to take possession of things.

172

NEVER DISPUTE WITH SOMEONE THAT HAS NOTHING TO LOSE

The fight will be unequal: the opponent enters the fight uncommitted, as they already have lost everything, even their shame. By letting go of everything, the competitor has nothing left to lose and plays with all the dirty weapons. Never expose your precious reputation to such risk. After all, it took you many years to acquire it and you can lose it in an instant, for an insignificant cause. A slight blowing of scandal is capable of freezing honored sweat. A good man knows how much is at stake, he knows what could harm his reputation. Therefore, he is cautious when making decisions, in order to safeguard his integrity. No victory recovers what was lost through disrespectful exposure.

173

DO NOT BE TOO SENSITIVE

Not even in friendship. There are people who fall apart over nothing, revealing how fragile they are. They become resentful and bother others. They are extremely sensitive, delicate like knick-knacks and cannot be touched, neither for fun nor seriously. They are offended by anything, they see the smallest speck of dust, even without a beam of light. Anyone dealing with a person like this must be very careful and never forget delicacy. The slightest insult affects them: full of themself, they are a slave to their own will, which overrides everything else, in addition to being a foolish idolater of their own sense of honor. The condition of a lover is half a diamond, in durability and resistance.

174

DO NOT LIVE IN A HURRY

If you organize your time, you will know how to make the most of it. For many people, they have too much time and not enough happiness, because they waste pleasant moments and then want to go back, they want to eat in one day what they could barely digest in a lifetime. They anticipate successes, devour the future and, since they are always in a hurry, they quickly conclude everything. Even in the desire for knowledge it is necessary to have moderation, so that things are not mislearned. We have much more time than obligations. Be quick to act, slow to appreciate. We enjoy much more satisfaction after accomplishing something than before doing it, but joy, once it is over, turns into sadness.

175

BE A TRUE
PERSON

Those who are true tend to be disillusioned with those who are not. Unhappyness is superiority that is not based on substance. Not all who appear to be true men really are. There are needy and incomplete people who feed on their own fantasies and give a false image. And there are others who prefer a fantasy, that is, they promise a lot and give little. Their successes and achievements have no basis, and their reputation is built on one lie after another. Only the truth builds a true reputation that, without a foundation, soon crumbles. One falsehood generates others, ending up generating promises in impossible deeds. Everything a liar promises is suspect, just as we suspect everything that seems too good.

176

KNOW HOW TO LISTEN
TO THOSE WHO KNOW

To live well, we need understanding, whether ours or borrowed. However, many people are not aware of their impotence, while others think they are wise, without being wise. There is no remedy for foolishness, since the ignorant, because they do not know their own ignorance, never look for what they lack. Some people would be wise if they did not believe they already are. Oracles of prudence, besides being rare, live idle, because no one goes to consult them. Asking for advice does not diminish greatness or testify against ability. On the contrary, it strengthens reputation. A good way to avoid misfortune is to listen to the voice of reason.

177

NEVER GET TOO CLOSE WITH OTHERS

Do not even allow them to get too close with you. You risk losing the superiority that integrity gave you and, with it, your reputation. The stars shine alone, divinity requires dignity, and familiarity can encourage disdain. Human relationships, when deepened, lose their charm, as close contact reveals the defects that reserve was hiding. It is not advisable to be very close with anyone; nor with superiors, as it is dangerous; nor with inferiors, as it is unworthy; and much less with the petty and insolent, as they are fools. Incapable of realizing that we are doing them a favor, they think that it is our obligation. Familiarity rhymes with vulgarity.

178

TRUST YOUR HEART

Listen and follow what your heart tells you. Typically, it knows what is most important: it is a personal oracle. Many perished from what they feared. If it was prevented, this would not happen. Some people have a very loyal heart, which always warns them, saving them from failure. It is not wise to go looking for evils, but rather to face them to overcome them.

179

SECRECY IS THE SEAL OF TALENT

A heart without secrets is an open letter. Reserve a place within yourself to keep your secrets: spaces and niches where important things can take refuge. Secrecy results from self-control, and being so is an authentic triumph. We pay the price when we reveal ourselves, the health of prudence consists of inner moderation. Those who probe us, who contradict us in order to manipulate us, or who induce even the most cunning of men to betray themself, threaten our reserve. Do not say what you are going to do, do not do what you say.

180

NEVER BE GUIDED BY WHAT YOUR ENEMY WOULD DO

The fool never thinks about doing what the cautious person does, as they have no discernment of what is appropriate. They will not do so, either, if they are discreet, in order to conceal their intention. Consider both sides of an issue before acting and try to remain impartial facing the possibilities. Do not think about what will happen, but about what could be.

181

DO NOT REVEAL THE WHOLE TRUTH

It is not always easy to tell the truth, as it can hurt your heart. It takes skill both to say it and to omit it. A simple lie can destroy the reputation of honesty: the deceived person is considered a fool, and, what is worse, the deceiver is considered false. Not all truths can be told: some must be kept for our own good, others for the good of one or more people.

182

SHOW A LITTLE BIT OF AUDACY

It is important to moderate the concept we have of others, so as not to praise them too much to the point of fearing them. Never allow your imagination to overlap your heart. Many people seem praiseworthy until we start to live with them. Conviviality usually brings more disappointment than admiration. No one can overcome the narrow limits of humanity, everyone has a flaw, either in character or talent. Social position confers apparent authority, but it is rarely accompanied by personal merit, as luck often punishes those in a high position by granting them less talent. Imagination always takes the lead and makes things seem better than they are. It conceives not only what exists, but what could exist. Reason, with the experience of disappointments, must see clearly and correctly. Fools should not be bold, nor should the virtuous be fearful. And if audacity is useful to fools, will it not help the wise and brave ones?

183

DO NOT BE STUBBORN

Fools are stubborn, and stubborn are fools. The more erroneous the judgment, the more they insist on it. A sensible man, when he realizes he made a mistake, admits it and gives in, thus demonstrating intelligence and dignity. One loses more by insisting than they can gain. Stubbornness in an opinion is not defending the truth, it is rude. Hard-headed people are difficult to convince, hopelessly obstinate. Whim and stubbornness, together, cause foolishness. Be firm in your will, not in your opinion. Obviously, there are exceptional cases in which one must not allow themself to lose so as not to be doubly defeated: in the trial and in the execution.

184

DO NOT BE CEREMONIOUS

Even in kings this affectation looks like eccentricity. Too much formality is uncomfortable. Some countries are affected by this ceremonial style. The clothes of fools, idolaters of their own honor, are sewn with these stitches and reveal that their character is based on little, as everything seems to offend them. It is important to have good manners, but not to play master of ceremonies. Of course, a person without ceremony needs great talent to do well, but courtesy should not be exaggerated or neglected. The one who sticks to trifles does not show greatness.

185

DO NOT RISK YOUR REPUTATION
IN A SINGLE MOVE

If the result is bad, the damage will be irreparable. It is common to make mistakes, especially on the first attempt. Remember that not every day is a lucky day. Therefore, allow a second attempt to make up for the previous error. If the first attempt is good, it will define the second one. There should always be room for improvement and appeal. Things depend on circumstances, and luck grants us success only once in a while.

186

KNOW HOW TO RECOGNIZE DEFECTS

The upright person must recognize any flaw, no matter how well disguised it appears, just like an object that, although plated in gold, cannot hide the rust. Defects may be coated with a layer of nobility, but none are intrinsically noble. There are people who notice a defect in someone they admire and respect, but they do not notice how this defect undermines their greatness. The superior example is so influential that it leads us to imitate even what is bad. Flattery imitates even an ugly face, without realizing that what is tolerable in superiors is unbearable in inferiors.

187

DO WHAT IS GOOD AND
IGNORE WHAT IS SORDID

With the first one we gain esteem, with the second one we avoid malevolence. Great men prefer to do good rather than receive it, they are happy to be generous. It is difficult to displease someone without displeasing yourself, out of pity or remorse, and the highest principles are motivated by reward or punishment. For the influence of good to be direct, and that of evil to be indirect, one must always have a shield against hatred and criticism. Anger is an animal instinct, without realizing the cause of the evil, it turns against the instrument, and the gag, although it is not to blame, takes the punishment immediately.

188

PRAISE THE ABSENT ONES

This is an attitude that reinforces your good taste, making others want your esteem. The person who recognizes perfection today will continue to recognize it tomorrow. Speaking well of others encourages conversation and imitation. It is a polite way of praising the qualities of those who are present. Some people do the opposite, or rather, always find something to criticize, flattering those present and disdaining those absent. This works with those who are superficial and are unaware of the ruse of speaking badly about each other. There are also those who value today's mediocrities more than yesterday's prodigies. A prudent man must be aware of these subtleties and not be influenced by excessive praise or resent their absence. The first one can be a tactic used indiscriminately, and the second one, a sign of caution and discretion.

189

MANIPULATION OF OTHERS' DESIRES

Deprivation, when it leads to desire, provides the most effective way to manipulate someone. Philosophers say that deprivation is nothing, while statesmen say it is everything: the latter are right. Some people climb up the steps of other people's desires to achieve their own goals, they take advantage of other people's difficulties, using them to stimulate their appetite. They consider lack more effective than the complacency of possession, because, as the difficulty increases, the desire intensifies. A subtle way to get what you want: keep others depending on you.

190

FIND CONSOLATION IN EVERYTHING

Everyone has a consolation, even the useless ones, because they are eternal. There is no evil that always lasts! For fools, consolation is luck. And luck is as the proverb says: "The beautiful ones would like to be as lucky as the ugly ones". To live a lot, you need to be worth little. The cracked glass does not break; we get sick of it, because it lasts so long. It seems that luck envies the most important people, rewarding uselessness with duration and importance with brevity. The great ones will always be few, and the ones that are useless, eternal. As for the unfortunate, luck and death seem to conspire to forget them.

191

DO NOT ACCEPT COURTESY AS PAYMENT

It is a kind of deception. There are people, to bewitch, they do not need magic potions; with the right gesture they enchant fools, or rather, the vain ones. They sell honor and pay debts with a stream of kind words. The one who promises everything, in reality, gives nothing; promises are traps for fools. True courtesy is a duty, false courtesy is a deception, and excessive courtesy is not dignity, but dependence. Whoever practices it reveres not the person, but wealth and flattery; not for good qualities, but for expected favors.

192

THE PEACEFUL MAN HAS A LONG LIFE

Remember: to live, let live. Whoever is peaceful not only lives, but also reigns. Listen and see, but keep silent, for a day without dispute is a night of rest. Living long and with pleasure is living twice: it is the fruit of peace. Those who do not worry about things that do not matter have everything. There is no greater foolishness than taking everything too seriously. Remaining open to what does not matter is as foolish as not getting involved with what really matters.

193

BEWARE OF ILL- INTENTIONED PEOPLE

The best defense to protect yourself from a smart person is attention. Against an expert, a good expert. Some make other people's business their own and, if we are not careful to always evaluate their intentions, we run the risk of being left behind.

194

BE REALISTIC AND DISCOVER POSSIBILITIES

Nothing falls from the sky without its own effort. This at any period of life. Many think highly of themselves, especially the most insignificant ones, and each one dreams of good luck and imagines themself a prodigy, harboring hopes that they cannot fulfill. The bigger the fantasies, the bigger the disappointment, so be sensible. It is positive to always wish for the best, but be prepared for the worst, as this will allow you to accept an adverse outcome with more serenity. It is good to aim high, but not so high that you miss the target. When starting a task, adapt your expectations. Where experience is lacking, mistakes are common. And prudence is the remedy for all foolishness. Everyone must know their capabilities and limitations. This way, you can adapt your imagination to reality.

195

KNOW HOW TO VALUE OTHERS

There is no one who cannot surpass someone at something, and there are always those who know more. It is useful to take advantage of what each person has to offer. The wise man appreciates everyone, as he recognizes the merits and qualities of each one. The fool despises everyone because they have no idea what is good and choose the worst.

196

KNOW YOUR GUIDING STAR

No one is so helpless as to not have one, and if you are unhappy, it is because you have not yet recognized it. Some have easy access to nobles and powerful people, without really knowing how or why, and the answer is simple: luck favored them, in addition to personal commitment. Others are graced with the gift of wisdom; some are more well-regarded in one country than others or are more successful in other cities. People with the same qualities and merits may have different activities or statuses. Luck plays its cards as and when it wants. The ideal is for everyone to know their potential and their guiding star and always follow it so that they never lose their way.

197

STAY AWAY FROM FOOLS

A fool is the one who does not recognize a fool and, even more, the one who recognizes them and does not get rid of them. Fools are dangerous in dealings and harmful in confidences. For a while, they are discreet out of their own caution or because of the care for others, but eventually they say nonsense or do stupid things. Those who do not have a reputation harm those of others. Fools are always unhappy, it is the burden they carry, and misfortune is contagious. They can only be useful as a lesson. These are examples of negative people.

198

KNOW HOW TO GO BEYOND

There are nations that only recognize their children after they venture out and stand out abroad. The homeland is like a stepmother to superiors, as envy finds fertile soil and reigns over everything, focusing on the imperfections of the beginning instead of the greatness achieved later. A mere pin gained appreciation as it traveled from the Old to the New World, and a glass bead made people despise the diamond. Everything that is foreign seems to have more value, either because it came from far away or because it is seen after it was drawn up and perfected. Some were despised in their homeland, but achieved worldwide fame. They are respected by their compatriots because they see them from a distance, and by foreigners because they came from far away. An image on the altar will never be venerated by someone who saw it when it was nothing more than a rough block of stone.

199

SEEK ESTEEM WITH CAUTION

Never try to force esteem. The best way to a good reputation is merit, and dedication, if based on value, it is the shortest way. Integrity alone is not enough, nor solicitude alone, which is unworthy, because with it things become so muddy that they can ruin one's reputation. Follow the middle way: have merit, but also know how to value yourself.

200

ALWAYS LEARN SOMETHING NEW

So as not to settle and become unhappy due to too much luck. The body breathes and the spirit aspires. If everything were achieved and obtained, we would only have disappointment and dissatisfaction. Even intelligence must always have something more to learn, a curiosity to satisfy. Desire gives us encouragement, but excess of happiness can be fatal. When rewarding others, never leave them completely satisfied. When they want nothing, we must fear everything: unfortunate luck. Fear begins where desire ends.

201

DO NOT BE FOOLISH BY THINKING YOU ARE WISE

Foolishness took over the world. If there is anything left of wisdom, it is foolishness in the face of divinity. The biggest fool is the one who does not see themself as such, only others. To be wise, it is not enough to appear, much less to appear wise to oneself. You show wisdom when you think you do not know, and you see when you think you do not see. Although the world is full of fools, no one considers themself one of them, nor are they afraid of becoming another one.

202

SAY WORDS AND DO WORKS

That is right: say what is very good and do what is very honorable. The first attitude reveals a superior mind; the second one, a perfect heart, and both are manifestations of a high spirit. Words are the shadows of works and acts. It is better to be praised than to praise others; it is easy to say and hard to do. Works are the substance of life, and words are the adornment.

Superiority endures in actions, but perishes in words. Works are the fruit of prudent reflection; moreover, words can be wise, and acts, heroic.

203

KNOW THE EMINENCES OF YOUR TIME

They are few. Great men appear once or twice in every century. Mediocre ones are common in quantity and value. Eminences are rare, as they require total perfection, and the higher the category, the more difficult it is to reach the top. Many called themselves "great," borrowing the names of Caesar and Alexander in vain. Without the deeds, the adjective is nothing more than a breath of air.

204

TREAT EASY THINGS AS HARD AND HARD THINGS AS EASY

The idea is not to get too confident or discouraged. For something to not take place, just consider it done. In moments of great danger, do not even think, simply act. Do not give importance to the difficulties and move on.

205

KNOW HOW TO USE DESPISE

A cunning way of getting things is by despising them. When you look hard for something, you do not find it. Later, when we already gave up, it appears without the slightest effort on our part. Earthly things are shadows of eternal things and behave as such: they run away when we pursue them and pursue us when we run away. Despise is the most political of revenge. A wise maxim is the one that says never to defend yourself with the pen, as this leaves a clue and glorifies rivals, instead of punishing them for their insolence. The unworthy ones cunningly oppose great men: they try to gain fame through indirect means, without actually deserving it. They would be unknown if their excellent opponents did not pay attention to them. There is no revenge more powerful than oblivion - bury others in the dust of their own insignificance. Only fools try to become immortal by destroying the wonders of the world and the centuries. A good way to silence vulgar talk is to ignore it, as contesting it causes harm and giving credit to it generates discredit. To discourage competitiveness, use complacency. A gold object placed in the shade does not lose its value, but it attracts less attention as it shines less.

206

KNOW THAT THERE ARE VULGAR PEOPLE EVERYWHERE

Even in Corinth and even in the most distinguished families. Everyone has tried it in their own home. Not only are there vulgar people, but there are well-born vulgar people, who are even worse. They reflect the qualities of the vulgar ones, like the shards of a broken mirror, but they harm more. They talk like fools and shamelessly criticize others; they are disciples of ignorance, godfathers of stupidity, eager for degrading talk. Do not pay the slightest attention to what they say, and even less to what they feel. Know them, yes, in order to get rid of them: avoid participating in their vulgarity or being the object of it. All foolishness is vulgarity, and vulgarity is made up of fools.

207

SEEK SELF- CONTROL

Stay alert, especially in the face of unforeseen events, as the impulses of passion unbalance prudence, and that is where the risk of getting lost lies. A single spark of fury or euphoria is more powerful than several hours of indifference. In a matter of seconds, we can do something that we will regret for the rest of our lives. The cunning spirit keeps a cautious prudence, in order to probe questions and penetrate the minds of opponents. By spying on secrets, they get to the bottom of the greatest talents. The counter-strategy is to control yourself, especially in emergencies. It takes a lot of reflection to stop a passion that can bolt like a horse. The one who foresees danger acts with caution. A word spoken in the impetus of passion may be insignificant to those who say it, but may be offensive to those who receive or evaluate it.

208

DO NOT DIE OF AN IDIOTIC ATTACK

Wise men often die mad. The fools, suffocated by advice. One dies of stupidity when they think too much. Some die because they feel everything, others live because they feel nothing. Some are fools because they do not die of feeling, and others are fools because they die of it. It is foolish to succumb due to excess of knowledge. Some succumb because they understand everything, while others live because they understand nothing. Although many die of foolishness, few fools actually die, for many do not even begin to live.

209

GET RID OF COMMON FOOLISHNESS

This requires common sense. Common foolishness is sanctified by habit. Those who withstood a certain ignorance were often unable to resist common ignorance. It is vulgar never to be content with ones own luck, even when it is the best, nor to be dissatisfied with ones own talent, even when it is the worst. Dissatisfied with their own happiness, they covet that of others. There are those who only praise the things of yesterday. The past seems better, and everything that is out of reach is more desired. The one who laughs at everything is as foolish as the one who grieves at everything.

210

KNOW HOW TO USE THE TRUTH

Even though the truth is dangerous, a good man cannot stop telling it. The skillful doctors of the soul invented a way to soften it, because when it causes delusion, it is the heart of bitterness. The task requires skill and correct procedure. The same truth can please some and offend others. To talk about the present, refer to cases from the past. When dealing with enlightened people, slight mentions are enough or, maybe, it is better to remain silent.

211

EVERYTHING IS JOY IN HEAVEN

Whereas in hell, everything is sadness. On Earth, which is in the middle, there are both things: we live between two extremes, and we share both. Luck changes, not everything is happiness and not everything is adversity. This life is a zero: by itself it is worth nothing, but added to heaven, it is worth a lot. It is prudent to remain indifferent to changes - wise people care little about news. Our life folds and unfolds, like a play, so be careful so that it ends well.

212

BE SUBTLE WHEN REVEALING YOUR ART

According to the great masters, they are always subtle in the way they reveal their subtleties. Thus, they maintain their superiority and mastery. Use art when revealing your art. Never exhaust the sources of teaching and revelation so that reputation and dependence are preserved. In teaching, as well as in pleasing, remember the ancient lesson: little by little revealing perfection and little by little gaining admiration. Discretion is an important quality for living and winning, especially in higher positions.

213

KNOW HOW TO CONTRADICT

This is a good ruse to probe others, as they commit themselves and we do not get involved in anything. Contradiction sharpens the passions of others. Showing disbelief encourages people to reveal their secrets. This is the key to closed hearts. With extreme subtlety, one can test the will and discernment of others. Sly disdain for a subject that someone involved in mystery will reinforce the impetus to bring it to light. Your reserve makes others lose caution and reveals their feelings, otherwise the heart would remain inscrutable. Pretending doubt is the best way to satisfy your curiosity: you will discover everything you want. Even in the learning process, it is a ploy for the student to contradict the master, who will strive to explain and substantiate the truth. Challenge someone discreetly and expand your learning.

214

DO NOT TURN ONE FOOLISHNESS INTO TWO

We usually made four errors to correct one. They say that one lie leads to a bigger one, and the same happens with foolishness. It is always harmful to support the wrong cause, even worse is not knowing how to hide the mistake. Imperfection charges its price, but we will pay even more if we defend and increase it. An oversight can make the greatest of wise men stumble, but if he knows how to use his other leg, he will regain his balance. If he does not know, he will fall for good.

215

BE AWARE OF SECOND INTENTIONS

The cunning man seeks to distract the other's will in order to attack them. He disguises his intentions to get what he wants and puts himself in the background in order to get there first. The shot hits anyone who is not careful. Stay alert until intentions become clear and thus you can perceive the trickery of those that are approaching. Watch the turns they take to get to what they want. They propose one thing and pretend another, that is, they move subtly until they reach the target of their intentions. Be careful with your concessions. Sometimes it is better to make others understand that you understood.

216

EXPRESS YOURSELF WITH CLARITY AND LUCIDITY

Some people think well, but express themselves poorly. Without clarity, the children of the soul - ideas, concepts and resolutions - never see the light. They are similar to those containers that hold a lot, but pour out little. While others, on the contrary, say even more than they feel. What resolution is to the will, explanation is to the understanding. Clarity and obscurity are two abilities: clear talents are praised, confusing ones are often admired for being incomprehensible. Sometimes it is good to be obscure in order to avoid vulgarity. However, how can anyone understand what they is hearing if the speaker does not have a clear idea of what they are saying?

217

DO NOT LOVE OR HATE FOREVER

Treat friends of today as if they could become your worst enemies tomorrow. Since this can happen, it is best to be prepared. Do not give ammunition to the turncoats of friendship; they would wage the worst type of war against you. On the contrary, when dealing with enemies, leave a door open for reconciliation, that of courtesy being the most indicated. The pleasure of revenge often turns into torment, and the satisfaction of having hurt someone into pain.

218

NEVER ACT OUT OF STUBBORNNESS

All obstinacy is negative, it is the result of passion, which makes more mistakes than it gets right. There are those who turn everything into war, cause social confusion and always think about defeating others in everything they do. People like that do not know how to live peacefully. They are particularly harmful for commanding and governing. They want to do everything stealthily and try to achieve things through intrigue. However, once their paradoxical spirit is discovered, they only manage to attract anger from others, who, contrary to what was intended, hinder their objectives even further. Normally, these people are unable to digest their own problems and become upset with everyone. They have an affected discernment, and even perverse hearts. The best thing to do is to stay away from people like that.

219

DO NOT BECOME KNOWN FOR ARTIFICE

Although it is almost impossible to live without it. It is better to be prudent than cunning. Everyone likes to be treated politely, but not everyone acts like that. Do not let sincerity turn into simplicity, nor sagacity into cunning. It is better to be worshiped as wise than feared as cunning. Sincere people are loved, but often deceived. The biggest artifice is to disguise the artifice, as it is taken as a hoax. Sincerity bloomed in the age of gold, and malice in this age of iron. It is an honor to be considered a capable person, as it inspires confidence. However, being seen as cunning raises the suspicion of sophistry and generates doubts.

220

WITHOUT THE LION'S SKIN, WEAR THE FOX'S SKIN

Life teaches that knowing how to give in in time is to exceed. The one who gets what they wants does not lose their reputation. In the absence of strength, use skill. Follow either of the two paths: the real one, of courage, or the shortcut of artifice. Dexterity accomplishes more than strength, and the wise ones have defeated the brave ones more frequently than the contrary. When you do not get what you want, you run the risk of being despised.

221

DO NOT BE PROVOCATIVE

In order to not compromise yourself or others. There are people who are extremely inconvenient, putting themselves in embarrassing situations and others as well. They are always one step away from foolishness, it is easy to find them and difficult to live with them. A hundred setbacks in one day are not enough for them. Everything annoys them and they contradict everyone and everything. With their common sense turned upside down, they disapprove of everything. However, those who most afflict our prudence are those who do nothing right and speak badly about everything. There are many people like that around us, do not be one of them.

222

MODERATE MAN, SIGN OF PRUDENCE

The tongue is like a wild beast: once released, it is hard to get it back into the cage. It is the pulse of the soul. The wise man uses it to diagnose our health; the attentive man, to listen to the heart. The problem is that the very person who should be most cautious tends to be the least cautious. The wise man avoids embarrassing, compromising situations and shows his self-control. He is circumspect, observant, vigilant. It would be better if Momo, the god of sarcasm and delirium, had wanted eyes in his hands rather than a window in his chest.

223

DO NOT BE ECCENTRIC

IRegardless of the situation, whether due to affectation or carelessness. Some have remarkable eccentricities and do extravagant things that are more defects than signs of distinction. Just as there are those who are known for a particularly ugly spot on their face, there are those who are known for a certain excess of mannerisms. Being eccentric will only draw attention to some unreasonable impertinence that will cause laughter in some and irritation in others.

224

KNOW HOW TO DEAL WITH THINGS

Even if they look bad. Everything has a face side and a reverse side. A knife can seriously injure whoever holds it by the blade or save the life of whoever holds it by the handle. Many things that caused pain would have caused pleasure, if their advantages had also been considered. There are always pros and cons. The secret is knowing how to turn things in our favor. They look different when seen in another light. So, look at them in the light of happiness. Do not confuse good with evil. There are always people who find joy in everything, and others only sadness. It is a good defense against setbacks of luck and a great rule of life, valid under any circumstances.

225

KNOW YOUR MAIN DEFECT

Everyone has some defect. You need to pay attention to it, identify it and then fight it. Otherwise, you will become a tyrant to yourself and others. Give this defect attention similar to that given by those who recognize and censor it. To be master of yourself, you need to reflect about yourself. Once this imperfection is mastered, all others will be mastered as well.

226

DO NOT COMPROMISE YOURSELF

Many people talk and behave according to the obligations imposed on them. They stop being what they really are and feel. Be careful: anyone can convince us of something bad. The best and most we have depends on the respect of others. Some are content with being correct, but that is not enough. It is necessary to be diligent, zealous. Pleasing others costs little and is worth a lot. With words you can buy works.

227

BE CAREFUL WITH FIRST IMPRESSIONS

There are people who cling to the first information they receive and pass everything else to the background. Normally, the lie is always the first to arrive. This way, there is no room for the truth. Do not satisfy your desire right away and analyze the first proposal carefully. Be perceptive! Some people are like new vessels for drink: they absorb the first aroma that reaches them, whether good or bad. The others, when they discover this limitation, start plotting with malice. The ill- intentioned paint credulity with the colors they want. Try to review things once, twice. Alexander, the Great, reserved his other ear for the other side of history. Pay attention to your second and third informants. Being easily impressed shows a lack of sagacity and is close to passion.

228

FORGET THE VOICE OF SLANDER

Do not become known for slandering others or being witty at someone's expense: this is very despicable. Everyone will take revenge and speak ill of you, and considering that you are one and the others are many, you will be defeated immediately. Do not get excited about other people's misfortunes, do not even comment on them. The gossiper is always detestable. It may deal with remarkable personalities, but they will value it as a source of fun, not prudence. And the one who says bad things hears even worse.

229

ORGANIZE YOUR LIFE WITH COMMON SENSE

And be careful to avoid physical and emotional wear. Life without rest is painful, as well as a long day of travel without rest. What makes life pleasant is the variety of learning. To have a beautiful life, take the first journey by learning from the dead ones: we were born to know, and know ourselves. And books faithfully transform us into people. Take the second journey with the living ones: contemplate and record all that is good in the world. Not all things can be found in one place. By distributing the dowries, the universal Father gave wealth to the less beautiful daughter. The third journey belongs entirely to you: philosophizing is the highest pleasure of all.

230

OPEN YOUR EYES IN TIME

Not all who see have their eyes open, not all who look are seeing. Perceiving reality too much does not bring relief, only grief. Some begin to see when there is nothing left to see. They lost their home and interests before finding themselves. It is difficult to instill understanding in someone without will, and even more difficult to instill will in someone without understanding. Those around them walk around like blind men, mocking them. Being deaf to advice, they do not open their eyes to see. There is no shortage of people who encourage this blindness: in order to be so, they depend on others not being so. Unhappy is the blind man's horse: it will hardly gain weight.

231

NEVER SHOW UNFINISHED THINGS

Dedicate yourself so that they are appreciated in their perfection. Every beginning is deformed, and the image of deformity is more striking and permanent. The memory of having seen something imperfect clouds our pleasure when it is complete. And contemplating a large object with a single look hinders our judgment about the parts, but satisfies our taste. Even the most delicious delicacy can cause repulsion while it is being prepared. Great masters take care that their works are not seen during creation. Learn from nature, and do not show yourself until you are presentable.

232

HAVE A LITTLE BIT OF A TRADER

Not everything should be speculation, action is needed. The wisest men are the easiest to deceive: they may know extraordinary things, but they know nothing about the common necessities of life. The contemplation of sublime issues diverts their attention from the mundane ones and, by demonstrating a lack of knowledge about the basic things of life, an area in which everyone else is so perceptive, they either fascinate or are considered ignorant by the majority. Therefore, let the wise man have a little bit of a trader, enough not to be deceived and ridiculed. Who knows how to achieve results: it may not be the highest concern in life, but it is the most necessary. What is the use, if knowledge is not practical? Currently, true knowledge lies in knowing how to live.

233

DO NOT CONFUSE OTHERS' ESTEEM

Many people cause pain instead of pleasure. Some try to please and end up annoying, because they do not understand the nature of others. The same thing that flatters some insults others, what was considered a favor turns into an offense. Sometimes, it would have taken less work to please than to annoy. Gratitude is lost and talent is ruined when one does not know how to please others. Without understanding someone's nature, you will not be able to satisfy it. It is one of the causes of misunderstandings, which are often irremediable; when you believe you are being pleasant, you are actually hurting. There are also those who think of flattering with eloquence, when in reality all they achieve is to annoy.

234

TAKE CARE OF YOUR OWN AND OTHERS' REPUTATIONS

The harm from talking too much and the benefits of silence must be reciprocal. When honor is involved, everyone must share the same interests, and one must care for the reputation of the other. It is better not to trust others, but if you do, do so with art, so that you make room for prudence and caution. Share the risk, so that you both pursue a common interest and so that your confidant does not become a witness against you.

235

KNOW HOW TO ASK FOR HELP

It seems simple, but it is not for everyone. For some, it is very hard. For others, easier. There are those who do not know how to say no. In this case, no stratagem is needed to deal with them. Others automatically say no, so you need to be more cunning. Approach them at the right time, surprise them when they are in a good mood, after delighting their mind or body. Unless, of course, they are paying close attention to your intention. Good days are ideal for getting favors, as joy flows from the inside to the outside. Do not bother people if they are angry or sad, because the problem that torments them will always be priority for them. Respect and wait for this worry phase to pass and then ask for help.

236

RETURN FAVORS

This is a trick of big politicians. Granting favors rather than just rewarding merit demonstrates nobility. Advance favors are even more rewarding because, in addition to arousing gratitude, they create a debt that becomes a moral obligation. This is a subtle way of inverting obligations, as what should be a reward for something done becomes an incentive to do it. This strategy only works among men of integrity and honesty. Among con artists, the advance reward acts more as a brake than a spur.

237

NEVER SHARE SECRETS WITH SUPERIORS

Many succumbed to trusting others with their secrets: by confiding, they became exposed and vulnerable. Hearing a prince's secrets is not a privilege, but a burden. Many break the mirror that reminds them of their ugliness, they cannot bear to see those who see them, and you will not be liked if you saw something unfavorable. Let no one owe us much obligation, especially the powerful ones. But if so, let it be more for the benefits we provide them than for the favors they did for us. Confidences to friends are the most dangerous of all. Whoever reveals their secrets to another becomes a slave, and such violence the sovereign cannot bear. In order to regain lost freedom, it will go beyond everything, even reason. Secrets? Do not reveal them and avoid listening to them.

238

DISCOVER THE QUALITY
YOU ARE LACKING

Many people would be complete if they did not lack some quality, a piece without which they will never reach perfection. Some could be much more if they paid attention to very little. Some lack dignity, which would make their qualities shine. Others lack delicacy, a flaw that directly affects friends, family and subordinates and that overlaps any positive quality. Others lack dynamism in using their qualities, while others lack serenity. All this lack, if noticed, could be easily corrected, as care can make the habit second nature.

239

DO NOT BE TOO PERCEPTIVE

Procure, antes, ser prudente. Se aguçar demais sua perspicácia, você perderá o ponto, ou o ultrapassará. É o que acontece com a astúcia comum. A verdade assentada é mais segura. É bom ter entendimento, mas não ser pedante. Muita argumentação constitui uma espécie de controvérsia, disputa. É preferível um critério substancioso que argumente apenas o necessário.

240

SIMULATE IGNORANCE

Sometimes even the smartest person uses this ruse. And there are occasions when the greatest knowledge is in appearing to have none. There is no need to be ignorant, just pretend. Wisdom is of little importance to fools, madmen care little about sanity. Therefore, speak to each person in their own language. The one who pretends to be is not a fool, for there is no foolishness where there is artifice. In order to be admired by others, wear a donkey's skin.

241

AVOID MAKING FUN OF OTHERS

Accepting a joke is a graceful demonstration, but practicing it can cause problems. The person who appears grumpy at a party is an even bigger beast than it appears to be. Well-made jokes are pleasant, knowing how to accept them is a sign of refinement. By getting angry or grumpy, you make others upset you again. The best thing is not to give it importance, and the safest thing is not to take notice about it. Many relationship problems arise from jokes, there is nothing that requires more attention and skill. Before starting, make sure how much the other's temper is capable of accepting.

242

BE PERSISTENT

Some start everything and finish nothing. Volatile in character, they start, but give up midway. They never receive praise, because they do not conclude anything. They even try hard, overcome difficulties, but they do not persist until the end. They demonstrate that they can, but they do not achieve victory. It is a defect, proof of inconstancy, of lack of discipline. If the undertaking is worth it, it is worth finishing. If not, why start? Wise men do not just stalk their prey, they go hunting.

243

DO NOT EXAGGERATE IN KINDNESS

May the cunning of the serpent alternate with the innocence of the dove. No one is easier to deceive than a good man; those who never lie and those who trust a lot, never deceive. Being deceived is not always a sign of idiocy; sometimes it reveals kindness. Two types of people prevent themselves from danger: those who learned at their own expense and those who are smart, who learned a lot at the expense of others. You have to be as cautious to foresee difficulties as you are cunning to escape them. Do not be so good that you give others the chance to be bad. Be part serpent, part dove; not a monster, but a prodigy.

244

INVERSION OF FAVORS AND VALUES

There are people who transform the favors they receive into their own merit: they give the impression that they are granting a favor when, in reality, they are receiving it. Some are so cunning that they grant honors when asking for a favor; and honor others for their own benefit. They arrange things in such a way that they seem to be donating when receiving something, reversing positions and casting doubt as to who favors whom. They get the best things only with praise. When demonstrating that they appreciate something, they do so in such a way that the other person feels flattered or privileged. They conjugate the verb to force in the active voice instead of the passive, they are better at politics than at grammar. This is great subtlety, but it is even more cunning to surprise someone practicing it: undo the exchange, reversing positions again and regaining the advantage.

245

ARGUMENT IN AN ORIGINAL WAY

This is proof of a superior talent. Do not think highly of someone who never opposes you, this attitude does not prove love or admiration - it shows that it loves and admires itself. Do not be fooled by flattery: do not reward it, condemn it. Consider it an honor to be criticized, especially by those who criticize good people. You should worry when your actions please everyone; this is a bad sign, as perfection is the privilege of a few.

246

DO NOT GIVE SATISFACTION TO THE ONE WHO DID NOT ASK

And even if they ask you, do not give them too much. Offering apologies before they ask for them is incriminating yourself; apologizing in advance awakens deeply dormant suspicions. Cautious people never hesitate when faced with the suspicions of others: that would be seeking offense. They try to disguise it with resolute and fair behavior.

247

KNOW A LITTLE MORE,
WORRY A LITTLE LESS

There are those who think the opposite. Good leisure is better than bad business. Time is the only thing that belongs to us, and an asset that everyone has, even those who have nothing. Life is too precious to be dedicated to overwork. Do not overwhelm yourself with occupations or disputes, as this is wasting your life and suffocating your spirit. There are those who extend this principle to knowledge as well, but those who do not know do not live.

248

DO NOT BE FICKLE

There are people who only believe the last information they heard. It is as if their senses and opinion were made of wax: each person who shapes them leaves their mark, erasing the others. They are easily influenced, like children who never grow up. Fickle in judgments and affections, they are always in flux, with opinions and discernment fluctuating, leaning this way or that.

249

DO THE ESSENTIAL FIRST

There are those who prefer to rest first and leave the effort and tiredness for later. Do the essential first and then, if there is time, the complement. Some want to win before fighting. Others begin their studies with what interests them least and postpone until the end of their lives what could bring them fame and benefit. Others become futile as soon as they begin to make a fortune. Having a method is essential to knowing and being able to live.

250

WHEN TO ARGUE BACKWARDS

For some people, everything is reversed: yes is no, and no is yes. If they criticize something, they actually admire it. Because they covet it for themselves, they try to devalue it in the eyes of others. Others avoid praising the good by praising the bad. The one who does not consider anyone bad cannot consider anyone good.

251

HUMAN MEANS AND DIVINE MEANS

Here is the advice, without comment, from a great master: use human means as if divine means did not exist, and divine means as if human means did not exist.

252

DO NOT LIVE ENTIRELY FOR YOURSELF

This is a common type of tyranny. Anyone who wants to be totally self-sufficient becomes selfish. Some people do not know how to give in, even in the smallest things, they do not give up even a minimum of their comfort. They never count on anyone's help, because they trust their own luck too much, giving them a false sense of security. It is good to need others from time to time, so that others need us too. Anyone who holds a public position must be a public slave - either carry the burden or give up the position - the saying goes. On the opposite, there are those people who dedicate themselves entirely to others, as foolishness always tends towards extremes, and this is a very unfortunate extreme. These are people who do

not have a day or hour for themselves, as they devote themselves completely to others. Even in intelligence and discernment, there are those who
know how to give the most sensible advice, but have no idea of their own
path. A person with common sense and balance helps others as much as
possible, without leaving aside their own interests.

253

DO NOT MAKE YOURSELF EASILY UNDERSTOOD

Most do not value what they understand and love what they do
not understand. To be valuable, things have to be difficult: by leaving
a hint of mystery in the air, you will be more admired and respected.
Sometimes it is useful to appear wiser and more prudent than necessary, but do it with moderation. Superior people duly value common
sense, but with the majority it is advisable to appear superior in some
way, so as not to give rise to criticism. Many praise what they cannot
understand. They venerate everything that is hidden or mysterious,
and they praise because they hear someone praising.

254

DO NOT BELITTLE AN EVIL BECAUSE IT IS SMALL

Remember that evil never comes alone, but always in a chain, just like
good luck. Generally, luck and bad luck are attracted, respectively, by the
positive or negative atmosphere. And everyone runs away from the un-
lucky and joins the lucky ones. Even doves, despite their naivety, fly to the
whitest tower. The unfortunate person has nothing: them are needy of
themself, their reason and any type of consolation. Do not awaken unhappiness when it is asleep, a stumble means nothing at first, but the final
fall can be fatal. Just as no good is complete, no evil is completely extingui-
shed. Face heaven-sent misfortunes with patience and earthly ones with
prudence.

255

KNOW HOW TO PRACTICE GOOD

Just a little at a time, but often. Do not grant more favors than they can return. Do not ask for thanks, because when the other party finds itself unable to reciprocate, it interrupts the relationship. To lose a lot, just force too much; in order not to have to return the favor, friends move away, turning into enemies. The idol does not want to see the sculptor who carved it. The one who receives a favor prefers to lose sight of the person who granted it. Therefore, learn this subtle lesson about giving: that it costs little and is desired a lot, so that it is more valued.

256

BE CAREFUL WITH ALL FOOLS

There are many types of fools: rude, stubborn, futile. Try to avoid them as much as possible. Arm yourself daily with the shield of prudence and, in this way, you will protect yourself from the moves of foolishness. Stay alert and do not risk your reputation on insignificant matters, those who are armed with common sense will not be attacked by inconvenience. Adjusting the course in human affairs is difficult, as it is like navigating rough waters, full of protruding reefs in which our reputation can run aground. The safest thing is to change course, following the example of Ulysses' skill, pretending a cunning carelessness. And, above all, use generosity and courtesy, which is the surest way to avoid complications.

257

NEVER BREAK UP DEFINITELY

Or your reputation will fall into pieces. It is easier to be an enemy than a good friend. Few are capable of doing good, and almost everyone is capable of doing evil. On the day it broke up with the scarab, not even the eagle felt safe nestled in Jupiter's chest. If you say something too abruptly, you will cause the anger of the hypocrites who were just waiting for the opportunity. The friends we hurt become our greatest enemies: to their own defects they add all ours. Others, when they see us break up with someone, say what they feel and feel what they want. They criticize our conduct either at the beginning of the friendship, for lack of prudence, or at the end, for having waited so long. If the only solution is to break up, let it be justifiable: better with fewer favors than with a violent explosion. Step aside with grace!

258

LOOK FOR SOMEONE WHO CAN HELP YOU TO ENDURE MISFORTUNES

This way you will never be alone, not even in risky situations, and you will not have to face the full burden of other people's hatred. Some people want to take control of everything themselves, and all they can do is be the only target of criticism. Therefore, always have someone who can help you to face adversity. Neither luck nor vulgarity dares to attack the two. The doctors, having failed in the treatment, make no mistake in consulting someone who can help them to carry the coffin. They share the weight and the grief, because enduring misfortune alone is doubly unbearable.

259

AVOID AFFRONTS

After all, it is wiser to avoid offenses than to take revenge on them. It requires great skill to turn a rival into an ally. Those who would have attacked your reputation become your protectors. It is very useful to know how to put others in debt to us. It leaves no time for insult who fills it with thanks. Transforming regrets into pleasures is knowing how to live. Make malevolence your ally!

260

KNOW WHO TO OPEN YOUR HEART TO

Blood ties are not enough, nor friendship nor even the strongest sense of obligation are enough. Giving someone your heart is very different from giving them your will. The most intimate union admits exceptions, which does not mean that the laws of courtesy are ignored. We do not tell all our secrets to a friend, nor does a son reveal everything to his father. We keep quiet about some things with some, and we talk to others and vice versa. There are things we can confess and others we need to retain. For each outburst, a different confidant.

261

DO NOT PERSIST IN FOOLISHNESS

There are people who start something wrong and insist on the mistake, because they consider it constant to do so. Deep down they recognize it, but in front of others they defend themselves. When they start with foolishness they are seen as reckless; when they continue, they are confirmed as fools. Neither a negligently made promise nor a mistaken resolution should bind us forever to a mistake. People who persist in making mistakes prolong their own stupidity and remain incompetent. They want to be faithful fools.

262

KNOWING HOW TO FORGET IS MORE A GIFT THAN AN ART

What we should most forget is what we remember most often. Memory is treacherous: it fails when we need it most and works when it should not. It is active when it can cause us pain and sloppy when it can give us pleasure. Sometimes the best medicine for evil is to forget, but we forget the medicine. It is therefore important to educate memory, as it can provide us with heaven or hell. Those satisfied with themselves are unaffected: in their foolish simplicity, they are always happy.

263

GOOD THINGS SEEM BETTER WHEN THEY BELONG TO OTHERS

Human beings tend to appreciate more what they do not have. On the first day, the pleasure belongs to the possessor, then to the others. When things belong to others, we appreciate them twice as much, for the pleasure of the novelty and the absence of the risk of losing them. Everything seems better when it does not belong to us; even other people's water looks like nectar. Possessing things, in addition to reducing the benefit, increases the annoyance, both by having to borrow them, and by denying them. When we have things, we actually keep them for others, and it is more enemies who demand permission to enjoy them than those who are grateful.

264

NEVER GET CARELESS

Luck likes to play tricks from time to time, and it will not miss the opportunity to catch you off guard. Intelligence, prudence, value and even beauty are always tested, as the slightest attention can lead to a fatal accident. The more cautious we need to be, the less we are, and not reflecting is a sure trap for failure. Cautious people carefully observe our qualities. Knowing the days of ostentation, cunning lets them pass. However, when we least expect it, we are put to the test.

265

EXERT YOURSELF AND OVERCOME YOURSELF

An effort, at the right time, transforms many into victorious people, just as the imminent threat of drowning creates swimmers. It was in this way that many discovered what they were worth and how much they knew, otherwise everything would have remained intact, with no result. It is difficult situations that give the opportunity to gain fame. And a noble person, when they sees their honor at risk, can do more than a thousand ones. This subtlety made great men.

266

DO NOT BE WEAK DUE TO EXCESSIVE KINDNESS

Getting angry is also necessary! Whoever feels nothing lacks personality. The fact that you never get angry is not a sign of insensitivity, but of incapacity. Reacting intensely, when circumstances require it, is a gesture of personal affirmation. Even the birds make fun of the scarecrows. Alternating bitter with sweet reveals good taste: sweetness alone is for children and fools. Being too good, after a certain point, constitutes a great evil.

267

SAY SOFT WORDS

The arrows pierce the body. The bad words, the soul. A good treat sweetens the mouth. Selling air is a subtle skill. Most things are paid for in words, and they alone accomplish the impossible. One negotiates in the air with the air, and the superior encouragement encourages more. You always need to have a mouth full of sugar to sweeten the words that even your enemies like. The only way to be kind is to be soft.

268

ACT AT THE RIGHT TIME

The cautious and the foolish do the same thing, the difference is in the moment. The former act at the right time, the latter at the wrong time. Whoever starts using intelligence backwards will do everything else in the same way. They crushes under their feet what they should have kept in their head. And more: they turn right into left and fail all the time. There is only one good way to see the light: as soon as possible. Otherwise, you will be obliged to do what you could have done with pleasure. The cautious person soon sees what has to be done sooner or later, and does it with pleasure, enhancing their reputation.

269

TAKE ADVANTAGE OF THE NEW

As long as it is new, it will be appreciated. The new pleases everyone because of the change; we feel our palate renewed. A new mediocrity is more appreciated than a known prodigy. Even what is excellent wears out and ends up getting old. Remember that the glory of new is fleeting, in a short time the respect you once had is lost. Take advantage of the first fruits of esteem and grab what you can, because once the heat of the novelty has passed, passions cool down, and pleasure turns into irritation. Do not forget that all things have their moment, and all things pass.

270

DO NOT CONDEMN ALONE

If something pleases many, there must be something good. And no matter how little you understand, value it. Eccentricity is always unfriendly; and when wrong, it is ridiculous. It discredits the person who criticizes more than the object criticized, and condemns the critic to be left alone with their bad taste. Anyone who cannot see the positive side of something that is venerated by everyone must disguise their limitations and not criticize with half words. Bad taste is often born from ignorance. What everyone says or is or wants to be.

271

IF YOU KNOW LITTLE, STICK TO THE SAFER

By acting this way, even if they do not consider you intelligent, you will inspire confidence. The one who knows can afford to take risks, but to take risks without knowing is to voluntarily throw oneself into a precipice. When we do not know the way, we do not leave the main road, because we do not know where the shortcuts lead. The tried and tested is always safe. No matter what it is, knowing or not knowing, safety is always more prudent than eccentricity.

272

SELL THINGS BY THE PRICE OF COURTESY

This way you will make others feel more obligated. The interested person's request will never reach as far as the generous person is willing to give, even if they owe an obligation. Courtesy does not simply give, but requires reciprocity. And delicacy is always well received. For a good man, nothing is more precious than what is offered for free. However, to petty men, delicacy is nothing more than palaver, for they do not understand the language of good manners.

273

KNOW THE NATURE OF THE PERSON YOU DEAL WITH

When we know the character of the people we interact with, we know their intentions. When you know the cause, you know the effect.

The effect reveals the reason to us. The negative person is always pessimistic, ominous; the slanderer only sees the defects. Those dominated by passion cannot see things as they are, as emotion overrides reason. Everyone expresses themself according to their nature and personality, and everyone is far from the truth. You need to know how to decipher the face to discover the features of the soul. Know that the one who always laughs is a fool, and the one who never laughs is false. Be careful with those who always question you, whether out of indiscretion or out of interest. Do not expect too much from ugly people or people whose physical appearance leaves much to be desired: they tend to want revenge on Nature for not having favored them. Foolishness is often directly proportional to beauty.

274

ATTRACTION IS A POLITICALLY COURTEOUS SPELL

May sympathy and courtesy captivate and win the goodwill of others, and also their favor. It is not enough to have merit if we are not liked, that is what makes us admired and praised, and acclaim is the most useful instrument we have to control others. Attracting sympathy can be a matter of luck, but it can also be promoted by artifice, which works best when combined with natural gifts. Sympathy leads to benevolence and, finally, to universal grace.

275

CONDESCENDING, BUT NOT INDECENT

Do not always appear serious or rigid: it is a matter of good manners. It is necessary to give in a little in decorum to win everyone's affection. Sometimes you can follow the path of the majority, but do it without losing your dignity: the one who is considered a fool in public will not be consider a wise person in private. More can be lost in a day of excessive relaxation than gained in years of seriousness. One should not always be exceptional, because to be eccentric is to condemn others. Even squeamishness in spiritual matters is ridiculous.

276

KNOW HOW TO RENEW CHARACTER WITH NATURALITY AND ART

A person's position changes with each cycle: may this change improve and elevate their taste. After the first seven years of life, we reach the age of reason; henceforth, may a new perfection be reached every seven years. Observe this natural mutation and promote it, and hope that others improve themselves, too. This is why many have changed their behavior, status or occupation. Sometimes you do not realize it right away until you see the blatant difference: at twenty years old, you are a peacock; at thirty, a lion; at forty, a camel; at fifty, a serpent; at sixty, a dog; at seventy, a monkey; and at eighty, nothing.

277

SHOW OFF YOUR QUALITIES

For each of them, there is a right time. Enjoy it; no one can triumph every day. There are certain people in whom, curiously, what is little shines brightly, and what is much, shines so brightly that it surprises us. When you have gifts and qualities to display, the results are phenomenal. There are nations that know how to dazzle - the Spanish do it better than any other people. As soon as the world was created, the light appeared to display it: ostentation satisfies, supplies what is missing and gives everything a second existence, even more so when it is based on reality. Heaven, which grants perfection, encourages us to show our gifts. Doing this requires skill; even the most excellent of men depends on circumstance, which is not always appropriate. Ostentation does not work out of season. Nor should we show off in an affected way, as ostentation borders on futility, which generates despise. We must exercise it with moderation, so as not to transform it into vulgarity. Among the wise men, exaggerated displays of gifts are not held in high esteem. It often involves a certain mute eloquence, a display of perfection as if by carelessness. Sensible dissimulation is the best way to gain admiration, as deprivation awakens curiosity. It requires skill not to reveal all the perfection at once, but to do it little by little, always adding. May each glorious occasion lead to another greater one, and may the applause given to the first one increase expectations for the following ones.

278

DO NOT DRAW ATTENTION TO YOURSELF

When people realize this attitude, qualities become defects. This arises from singularity, which was always censored: the eccentric is always abandoned. Even beauty, if it is excessive, is unfavorable, and if it is noticed, it offends, especially when displayed without tact. Even intelligence, if strutted, is interpreted as bravado.

279

DO NOT ANSWER TO THOSE WHO CONTRADICT YOU

Make sure first whether the person is perceptive or simply vulgar. It is not always a matter of difference of opinion or even stubbornness; sometimes it is a ruse. So, be careful and do not let yourself be caught by the first one, nor get discouraged by the second one. No one demands more caution than a spy, and when it comes to someone who prepares traps for minds, protect yourself by locking it with the key of caution.

280

BE AN HONORABLE MAN

Good manners are rare these days, debts of gratitude are not respected, and few give others the treatment they deserve. The most important services are the least rewarded; this is the custom all over the world: there are entire nations inclined to treat foreigners badly. From some, betrayal is feared; from others, inconstancy and also achievement. Pay attention to other people's bad behavior. Not to imitate it, but to defend yourself from it, as your own integrity can be ruined by the disastrous conduct of those around you. The honorable man, however, does not forget who he is, thanks to what others are.

281

GAIN THE APPROVAL OF IMPORTANT PEOPLE

The indifferent yes of an extraordinary man is worth more than the enthusiastic applause of the common crowd. Why rejoice with the villagers' outbursts? The wise men speak with understanding, and their praise provides immortal satisfaction. The judicious Antigonus reduced his audience to Zeno alone, and Plato considered Aristotle his entire school. Some people just want to gorge themselves on flattery, even if it is vulgar in origin. Even sovereigns need someone to write about them, and they fear pens more than the ugly ones fear the artist's brushstrokes.

282

TAKE ADVANTAGE OF ABSENCE

To gain respect or esteem. Presence diminishes fame, absence increases it. The absent person who was considered a lion, when present turns into a mouse. Treats lose their shine when touched: you see the outer shell and not the spiritual core. Imagination travels faster than vision. Achievement enters through the ears, but generally comes out through the eyes. The man who withdraws into himself, into the core of his reputation, preserves his good name: even the phoenix uses absence to preserve dignity and transforms desire into appreciation.

283

BE CREATIVE, BUT
WITH COMMON SENSE

Creativity reveals extreme intelligence, but who can have it without a touch of madness? Creative people are original; those who choose wisely are prudent. Creativity is also a grace, and very rare, since many are good at choosing, but few are good at creating with common sense, and these few were the first ones, in excellence and time. Novelty is attractive and, when successful, makes what is good shine even brighter. In matters of discernment, creativity is dangerous, as it involves the eccentric; in matters of intelligence, it is praiseworthy, and, when right, both deserve applause.

284

TAKE CARE OF YOUR OWN LIFE

To always be respected. Esteem yourself if you want to be esteemed, be ambitious with yourself, not prodigal. Go where you are wanted and welcome, but never come unless called, nor ever go unless sent. A man who commits himself on his own initiative, when he fails, attracts aversion upon himself and, when he succeeds, he receives no gratitude. The meddler is an object of despise; getting involved where he should not, he will be rejected and repelled.

285

DO NOT SINK WITH OTHERS

Know those that are stuck in the mud and wait that they will look for you, seeking for help and mutual comfort. Unhappiness needs company, and unhappy people extend their arms to those they once turned their backs on. Be careful when trying to save someone who is drowning. You cannot save them without putting yourself in danger.

286

DO NOT OBLIGATE YOURSELF TO EVERYTHING, OR TO EVERYONE

For that would mean being a slave, and of everyone. Some people are born more fortunate than others; they may do good, while others receive it. Freedom is more precious than the gift that makes us lose it. It is better for many to depend on us than for us to depend on just one, and the only advantage of having power is being able to do greater good. Above all, one should not take an obligation imposed by others as a favor. Most of the time, it was the wit of others that put them in such a position.

287

DO NOT BE MOVED BY PASSION

We cannot answer for ourselves when we are not reasoning well, and passion always overrides reason. Therefore, find a prudent third party, indifferent to passion. Spectators always see more than players. When prudence feels the approach of a strong emotion, it is time to retreat. Otherwise, your blood will boil, and a brief explosion could result in several days of discomfort for you and slander for others.

288

LIVE ACCORDING TO THE CIRCUMSTANCES

Dominating, arguing, everything must be done at the right time. Do things when you can, because time and opportunity wait for no one. Do not live according to generalities, unless it is a question of acting with virtue, nor expect your will to follow precise rules, because tomorrow you may have to drink the water you despised today. There are people so impertinent that they paradoxically expect circumstances to adapt to their whims, helping them to do well, instead of the other way around. However, the sensible ones know that prudence consists in acting according to the occasion.

289

A MAN'S GREATEST DISADVANTAGE IS SHOWING THAT HE IS HUMAN

Others stop seeing him as divine from the moment they start to see him as human. Frivolity is the biggest obstacle to prestige, those who are reserved are considered superior, while those who are frivolous are considered inferior. No addiction is more degrading, for it is totally opposed to respectability. A frivolous person cannot have any substance, even less in old age, as age demands prudence. And such a defect, although common, can lead to irremediable disgrace.

290

DO NOT UNITE APPRECIATION AND AFFECTION

If you want to be respected, do not be loved too much. Love is bolder than hate, affection and veneration do not mix. Be neither too feared nor too loved, as love leads to intimacy and undermines respect: be loved with admiration rather than with affection.

291

KNOW HOW TO TEST OTHERS

May attention and common sense penetrate seriousness and reserve. It is necessary to have a great power of discernment to evaluate others, and it is more important to know the qualities and tempers of people than the properties of stones and herbs. This is one of the most subtle things in life - metals are identified by sound, and people are identified by speech. Words reveal integrity, actions even more. It is necessary to have extraordinary care, deep observation and critical capacity.

292

NATURAL ABILITY MUST SURPASS WORK DEMANDS

No matter how high or prestigious the position, always show that you are greater. The talent that has reserves expands and becomes more obvious with each activity: those who have a narrow mind and a petty heart are easily surprised, and, in the end, the weight of obligations ends up crushing their reputation. The great Augustus prided himself on being a better man than a prince: you need to have greatness of spirit and also solid confidence in yourself.

293

MATURITY

It shines in a man's exterior, and still more in his habits. Material weight gives value to gold, and moral weight gives value to a person; it is the refinement of qualities, which causes veneration. Composure is the facade of the soul; it does not constitute the insensitivity and tranquility of fools, as the futile believe, but a confident sense of authority. Maturity is shown through wise words and thoughtful attitudes. A man is considered mature when he has both humanity and maturity and, as he stops being a child, he becomes serious and judicious.

294

MODERATE YOUR JUDGEMENTS

Each person forms ideas according to its interests, and presents plenty of reasons to defend them. In most people, discernment yields to emotion. It is common for two adversaries to face each other, both convinced that they are right. However, the reason is true, and it never has two faces. In this type of confrontation, the wise man proceeds with reflection: from time to time, he considers the other side and, carefully, reevaluates his own opinion. Analyze your motives from the other person's point of view, this way you will neither condemn it nor justify yourself blindly.

295

BE A MAKER

Those who are most proud of their achievements are those who have the least reason to be. They turn everything into a mystery, and they do it with the greatest negligence: they are applause hunters, always in the center of the arena. Vanity was always boring, but with this type it is ridiculous. They go begging for exploits, little ants accumulating honors. One must show the slightest vanity of their own talents. Be content with doing: leave the comments for others. Offer your achievements, do not sell them: try to be heroic instead of just appearing so.

296

HAVE MAJESTIC TALENTS

Great talents make great men, and an exceptional quality overcomes an abundance of mediocrity. There have been those who wanted all their things to be great, including common utensils, but the great ones must strive for high spiritual qualities. In God, everything is infinity, huge; and, therefore, in a hero everything must be great and majestic, so that their actions and even their words can be clothed with great and transcendent majesty.

297

BEHAVE YOURSELF AS IF YOU WERE OBSERVED

The man who is attentive to his actions knows that others see him, or will see him. He knows that walls have ears, and that what is wrong will soon be discovered. Even when he is alone, he behaves as if the whole world was watching him, because he knows that everything will be revealed. Now consider as witnesses those who, through communication, will become witnesses later. The man who wants everyone to see his house does not mind that it is scoured.

298

THREE THINGS MAKE A PRODIGY

And they are the high point of true nobility: fertile intelligence, deep discernment and good taste. Imagination is a remarkable gift, but it is even more admirable to reason well and understand good. Intelligence must be sharp, not laborious. It should reside in the head, not the spine. When you are twenty years old, your will rules; at thirty, intelligence; at forty, discernment. Certain brilliant minds radiate light, like the eyes of a lynx, and reason better in the dark. Others always discover what is most relevant. Solutions come to them easily and in the right way: a fortunate fruitfulness! As for good taste, it gives flavor to their entire life.

299

NEVER QUENCH

Always leave a little bit of nectar on their lips. Appreciation is proportional to desire. As with thirst, it is good to relieve it, but not to quench it. Everything that is good, if it is little, is twice as good. The first sip is the best of all, the second one is good, the rest do not even compare to the first one. Exaggerated satisfaction makes the object of desire lose its value. The most important rule to please is to sharpen their appetite, not completely satiating it. The impatience of expectation is more stimulating than the satiety of desire. Waiting intensifies the pleasure.

300

BE A SAINT

Virtue is what links all perfections, the core of all happiness. It makes a person prudent, discreet, perceptive, sensitive, sensible, brave, cautious, honest, happy, praiseworthy, true; in short, a full universal being. Three things make us blessed: holiness, wisdom and prudence. Virtue is the sun of the lower world, its hemisphere is good awareness. It is so charming that it wins the grace of God and others. There is nothing so lovely as virtue, nor so detestable as addiction. Virtue alone is authentic; everything else is imitation. Talent and greatness depend on virtue, not luck. Ability and greatness are measured by virtue, not by luck. Only virtue is enough in itself. It makes us love the living and remember the dead.

www.ingramcontent.com/pod-product-compliance
Lightning Source LLC
LaVergne TN
LVHW060353200726
843506LV00003B/206